A CENTURY IN THE MAKING

A CENTURY IN THE MAKING

A HUNDRED-YEAR JOURNEY FROM REFUGEE TO AMERICAN

PETER LINDENFELD

FLARE BOOKS
El Paso, Texas

Published by Flare Books,
an imprint of Catalyst Press, El Paso, Texas
www.catalystpress.org

In North America, this book is distributed by
Consortium Book Sales & Distribution, a division of Ingram.
Phone: 612/746-2600
cbsdinfo@ingramcontent.com
www.cbsd.com

First edition, first printing
1 3 5 7 9 8 6 4 2

ISBN 9781963511321 (paperback)
ISBN 9781963511338 (ebook)
Library of Congress Control Number: 2025936333
Cover design by Aaron Petrovich

TABLE OF CONTENTS

"There are things in your life that only you will see, stories that only you will hear. If you don't tell them or write them down, if you don't make the picture, these things will not be seen, these things will not be heard." – Emmet Gowin, photographer. From a lecture on the occasion of his retirement from Princeton University, October 24, 2009. Quoted in Emmet Gowin, Fundacion Mapfre, Instituto de Cultura, Madrid, Spain, published in association with Aperture Foundation 2013.

* * * * *

"Budda's Box" by Vida Chu

A man died. Just as he realized how short his life was, he saw Buddha coming toward him holding a box in his hands.

"We must go," Buddha said.

"So quick?" said the man. "I have a lot of unfinished things."

"Very sorry," said the Buddha. "But your time is up."

"What's inside your box?" the man asked.

"It is your legacy," said Buddha.

"My legacy? You mean my clothing and my money?" said the man.

"Those things were never yours," said Buddha. "They belong to the earth."

"Are they my memories?" the man asked.

"No," said Buddha. "They belong to time."

"Are they my endowment?" the man questioned.

"No," said Buddha, "that belongs to circumstances."

"Could it be my friends and family?"

"No," said Buddha. "They belong to the journey that you took."

"My wife and children then?" the man said.

"No, they belong to your heart," said the Buddha.

"Then it must be my physical body?" asked the man.

"No, your body belongs to dust," said the Buddha.

Decisively the man said, "It must be my soul."

Buddha smiled and said, "Child, you are mistaken, your soul belongs to me."

With tears in his eyes the man took the box from Buddha and opened it. It was empty. With tears streaming down his face and his heart shattered, he asked, "Could it be that I have never owned a single thing?"

"Yes," said Buddha. "In this world nothing really belonged to you."

"Then what was mine?" asked the man.

Buddha said, "When you were alive, each moment belonged to you."

PREFACE

My 13th birthday was on March 10, 1938. I have no memory of it because it was overshadowed by the events of the next day, that of the *Anschluss*, the annexation of Austria by Germany. I remember standing at the window of our apartment, looking at the surrounding buildings that were now covered with the red flags showing the swastikas symbolic of the Nazi regime.

Crowds of people were marching, singing, and shouting slogans such as *Ein Volk, Ein Reich, Ein Führer* (one people, one state, one leader). The swastika pins that had been illegal before that day were now everywhere.

My parents' reactions represented two sides of the Jewish community. My father said "this can't last" and made no move. My mother concentrated on finding a way to leave. I was her only child, and seeing me safe was a major motivation for her. She had always been the stronger and the more forward-looking member of the family, and she succeeded in saving herself and me, and eventually also my father. He was one of five siblings, and two of them died in the camps that were established to exterminate the Jews. There is little doubt that, without my mother's efforts, this would also have been his fate.

Where was I amid the turmoil? My childhood was at an end, but what was next? I was buffeted by the events, but I had no way to influence them. I did what was expected of me, trying to fit in as best I could.

After some time, my mother and I were able to leave the country. Everything from then on was unfamiliar. My life was no longer orderly and predictable. I became a refugee and never again lived in a country where the only language that I knew then was spoken. Still, I did not feel alienated or abandoned. I lived in the present without knowing or considering what would come next.

When I tell people of my writing this book, they say, "Oh, you're writing your memoir. That's good. You need to do it for your children."

That's not what I am doing here. Most who know me already know the outlines of my life, as well as some of the day-to-day happenings that have formed the stories that they have heard repeatedly.

My motivation is different. Is it foolhardy to think that I can illuminate some of the spirit of the time? Many have done that. Can I use the personal to go beyond that which is mine alone?

One of my favorite radio programs is *Music You Can't Hear on the Radio*, hosted by John Weingart on WPRB, Princeton. It consists mostly of folk songs, a blend of the well-known and the unexpected, loosely built around themes, but not bound to a fixed pattern. Sometimes the same piece is repeated with different performers, instruments, or arrangements. There is the warmth of recognition of the familiar, and the illumination of new sounds and new thoughts. Is it presumptuous to think that I can adopt some of these features?[1]

Being a refugee shaped my life. I became more aware of others, those who helped my family and me, those who shared our fate, and those who had a much more difficult time. Almost all the people whom I met came from different cultures, with different backgrounds and experiences. My eyes were opened to a world beyond the one which I had known—startling, surprising additions that I could not have predicted. The future would come, one piece at a time, each moment a boundary between the known past and the unknown to come.

The illusion of stability: My mother in the Praterallee, Vienna 1937

PART 1: THE ILLUSION OF STABILITY

VIENNA

There was a coal bin in the kitchen. On the wall was a shelf with three jars, one labeled "sand" and one "soda." What was the third? Some kind of soap, used to clean pots like the other two?

I liked to sit there in the corner. It was cozy, and I felt protected. My parents worked and I was supervised by maids, a succession of young women from the country who took me for walks and gave me my food. They were a constant presence, intimate and at the same time separate and remote. I was aware of their limited authority.

Before I went to school I mostly played alone. I remember stone blocks and other construction toys. I had a teddy bear that my father gave away without telling me when he thought I was too old for it.

Before that was the time of the *Lutscher*, the pacifier, a source of comfort, but also of guilt and disgust, as I sucked on it. I'm told that the time came when I looked at it, said "pfui," and threw it away.

When I was five or six years old, my parents made a number of alterations to the apartment, adding a corner for me in the living room, with a small table, chair, and bookshelf. That was my space. That's where I lived. Modern pieces replaced the old dining table and cupboard. Their clean, unadorned lines, replacing the fussiness of the previous century, still represent the taste and design that I favor.

My father wrote letters on small square cards, elaborate designs in blue and red, and I learned to read. Later, when I was asked what I learned from him, this is what came to my mind.

Were there other children? I remember only my cousins before I went to school. In my first year of public school, only a few minutes' walk away, I remember none of my fellow pupils. I see the teacher vividly, a not unkindly man, standing in front of the class, with us, the 40 children, sitting quietly, with our hands folded or flat on the desks.

The next school was different, the *Schwarzwaldschule*. It had been a girls' school, a landmark in the history of women's education, started by the woman (Eugenie Schwarzwald) whose name it carried. It was the first girls' school in Austria that led to the university entrance exam, the *Matura*, and also acted as a bridge from the terminal school to which most girls went. That's where my mother had gone, and it opened the world for her. Now it included an elementary school, and I went there for the next three years.

It was a progressive school with small classes in bright rooms, a lively spirit, and an encouraging atmosphere.

I remember just two classmates that I saw outside class, gangly Ingmar and Lisbeth with her apron. The only other person that I remember is the principal, *Oberlehrerin* Reiss. As a special reward she would occasionally paste a picture or postcard in our *Arbeitsbuch* (workbook). Each student had one, a bound notebook into which short essays, quotations, and poems were copied from time to time. She said that students generally kept theirs all their lives. I had mine for some decades. Now it is lost.

My other memory of the Oberlehrerin is from the time

when she came to the classroom during school hours and asked that I come out. Some days earlier I had been in the *Stadtpark* (city park) with my mother. You weren't allowed to walk on the grass, which was separated from the walkway by a low scalloped metal border. I was walking along it with one foot inside and one outside, straddling the border, when a policeman stopped me. He berated me, and with a show of officious authority wrote out a report describing my misdemeanor. I was terrified by this confrontation, but had forgotten it by the time Frau Reiss called me out to tell me that she had received a copy of the report in the mail. I can hardly imagine that she took my crime seriously, but there was no hint of irony in her voice as she gave me a lecture on the importance of obeying the law.

A half-century later, in a small town in Germany, I was walking along a narrow, almost deserted street. When I saw a policeman on the other side, I crossed over to ask him for directions. Before I could say anything, he erupted in accusations: It was forbidden to cross in the middle of the block. The memory of the earlier encounter, with its vehement response to a trivial infraction, came back to me.

Where is the borderline between an orderly environment and a police state? It is difficult to legislate flexibility and discretion, but can we do without them? Could there have been a more humane reaction, proportional to the offense? Automatic condemnation and punishment are simpler, but that's where oppression starts.

* * * * *

My only close family members were my mother's sister Alice (pronounced the Italian way, as Alittsche), whom I called *Tante* Litschi, her husband, Willy, and their two daughters, who were the closest approximation to siblings for me. The older one, Erika, was a willful, rebellious child, overshadowed by her brighter, more appealing sister, Renate.

Renate was three years older than I. I loved her, but whether I was five, eight, or ten, she was always unattainably more grown-up, mature, in a world beyond my reach. My mother would have private talks with her from which I was excluded. I had no idea what they were about, but surely, they were about a more adult life, only dimly perceived by me, but reeking of the forbidden, the hidden, the sexual.

Our two families got together more or less formally each year for the Passover holiday at my grandmother's apartment. Everyone sat around the large table and my father and Uncle Willy mumbled through the Hebrew text. As the youngest, it was my duty to ask the four questions that are central to the program, and lead to the recounting of the history of the oppression of the Jews and their leaving Egypt in the original Exodus. I did this haltingly, reading the phonetic Hebrew, without any knowledge of the meaning of the words or of what I was saying.

The festive table, the ritual, the warmth of family, made this a cherished occasion. For once, there was food that I liked, such as the *charoset*, the sweet mixture of nuts and apples that is meant to remind us of the mortar that the Jews used in the time of their slavery. The main course was always the same: cold jellied carp. It was full of bones, and Renate and Erika assured me that if I swallowed even the tiniest one, it would get stuck in my throat and I would die. I liked the once-a-year fish, and their exaggerated warning didn't keep me from eating it. However, with the extreme care that I took to avoid the bones, I was always the last to finish.

Other meals were rarely a source of pleasure. My parents and I sat around the small round table in our living room, served by the maid. They talked about hospitals, patients, diseases, bloody mishaps. I was both fascinated and repelled. Perhaps this kind of conversation turned me toward the inanimate sciences.

I was a bad eater. I dawdled and stared at food I didn't like and made no attempt to eat it. Sometimes my father stormed off, shouting, "I can't watch this anymore!" One time I was horrified by a piece of liver whose very appearance made me nauseous. I was told I would get nothing else until I had eaten it and wouldn't be allowed to get up from the table until then. I finally put a piece in my mouth but couldn't get myself to swallow it. I sat at the table with the liver in my mouth until, sitting there alone, I finally had the courage to take it out and throw it away.

No doubt my eating habits had psychological origins as I tried to revolt against my environment and draw attention to myself, but today I would still find much of the food unpalatable. Vegetables were boiled to destruction and served with a thickening of flour and butter. Globules of fat covered soups, eggs were runny, meat was overdone, tough and tasteless, often consisting of organs like the liver that aroused such revulsion in me.

Vienna was and still is famous for its desserts. On special occasions we would go to a pastry shop where I would be served one of these concoctions, generally buried under a mountain of whipped cream. I must have overdosed, because in later life I have rarely been tempted by rich desserts.

I was back in Vienna just once, decades later in 1984, this time with Lore, my wife. My memories of the earlier time were detailed and vivid, but people who had been there said that everything had changed so much that I would recognize nothing. That's not what I found. There were changes in the touristy sections in the center of the city but the rest was largely as I remembered it. The apartment house on the *Hernalser*

Hauptstrasse was unchanged, except that the *Bierstube* (bar) next to the building's entrance had been replaced by a bakery. My father had occasionally sent me down from our apartment with a mug to get beer for him. I was disgusted by the yellow liquid. When I told him years later that I never once tasted it, he was surprised. He clearly expected me to be more independent. I had tried hard to do what I thought was expected of me, and realized only later that always doing what you're told is not only a way to become boring and uninteresting, but it is not even particularly valued in the grown-up world.

There was still no elevator and we walked up. The stairs went back and forth, with "half-floors" between the floors. I don't know whether there were still the shared toilets facing the hallway on the half-floors as I remembered them, but didn't investigate. Outside the door of our former third-floor apartment, the tiled floor with the Roman design was unchanged. That's as far as we went. I thought briefly about the fate of our home, taken over by the maid when we left.

On the way out we got some *Topfengolatschen* from the bakery. The sensual experience brought back more memories. The closest term that I can think of is "cheese Danish," but neither the sweet filling of cottage cheese and raisins, nor the flaky crust that made each bite a thrilling experience, resembled anything that I have ever seen on this side of the ocean.

* * * * *

The richness of Viennese culture and its food were largely the result of the city's former status as the capital of the Austro-Hungarian empire. Baked goods such as the sweet *Golatschen* and squarish *Buchteln*, the round *Semmeln* that carried the imprint of the hands that shaped them, and moon-shaped *Kipfel* were reminders of that time. Often the names were adapted from the Czech and the Polish, the Hungarian, the Romanian, the Serb and the Croat, reflecting their origins in the provinces of the Empire.

The citizens of Vienna are brought up to consider themselves the saviors of Christendom, besieged by the Turks in 1529 and again in 1683, the only dates of Vienna's history that have stayed with me since school. We were taught that later developments would have been very different if the invaders had not been rebuffed. The Viennese learned about coffee at that time, and continued to be influenced by their position in the easternmost capital of Western Europe, on a peninsula jutting into the Slavic regions to the north and south and Hungary to the east.

When two former Viennese meet, they go through a kind of dance as they talk about common experiences and acquaintances. It usually starts with "Which *Bezirk* (district) did you live in?" There were 21 then, and where you lived said a lot about who you were.

In the center is the "inner city" with the *Stefanskirche* (Saint Stephen's cathedral) as its most visible and symbolic structure. It is bounded by the *Donaukanal* (Danube canal) and the *Ringstrasse*, the broad avenue with its public buildings such as the Parliament, the City Hall, the Emperor's Palace, and the twin museums of art and natural history.

A second concentric shell consists of the bourgeois districts. Its outer boundary is the *Gürtel* (belt), at that time distinguished by its elevated tramway. Museums, hospitals, and stores are imbedded in a sea of apartment buildings. There are further gradations of class and I was aware that the third district was more elegant, but I didn't know anyone there, and it was outside my walking area.

This group of districts does not include the second district, at that time a ghetto-like area, primarily the home of Jews from eastern Europe, many with beards and black kaftans. They spoke Yiddish or German with a thick accent, and represented what my parents wanted to escape: the darkness and superstition, the medieval, the Diaspora, when Jews were segregated and oppressed. When I said something hinting at the lilting Eastern speech I was admonished, "*Jüdel nicht!*" (Don't speak with this Jewish accent) Yiddish, with its German roots but distinct features, with its adaptations from Hebrew and European languages, was not even thought of as a separate language by assimilated Jews like my parents. They saw it only as a perversion of German. I was seldom in the second district, and it was rare to see someone with the typical black clothing in another part of the city.

* * * * *

There was no doubt that we were Jews. Everyone in the family was conscious of it and we never denied it. There was frequent talk of the common discriminations, such as the quotas that were applied formally or informally, especially for government and university positions, as well as in the commercial world. These exclusions led to the prevalence of Jews in professions such as medicine and law where they could be independent. My father would mention physicians who had contracts with the health insurance system, which led to a stream of patients and higher earnings from which he was excluded.

The majority of people my parents saw socially were Jews. Some had been baptized and become nominal Christians as a step toward assimilation and as an attempt to escape the ever-present, pervasive anti-Semitism. They hoped that this would help their children pass into a world free of the constraints suffered by them. Often it was accompanied by a change of name from a typically Jewish one. They could not know that within a short time these moves would prove useless as shields from the coming assaults.

During our last year in Vienna my parents discussed becoming *getauft*, christened. I was adamantly opposed. That was not because of some affinity for Jewish beliefs and practices, of which I knew little. I saw it primarily as something that would take away my identity and would rob me of a core portion of who I was. I did not choose to be a Jew. It was something that I was and that helped to define me.

Jews were generally made to feel that they were outsiders. It is not surprising that this led me to want to belong, to be part of a larger entity, a bigger family, a larger community. At the same time, I have refused to join groups that seemed to require me to give up or compromise some belief or practice that was important to me. I have often felt shut out, unable to penetrate a real or imagined barrier. To cease to be a Jew would have meant to be adrift in a world of which I knew nothing, to be a rootless pretender, forever alien. This choice may have marked the first time that I asserted my independence. In most situations I remember only acceptance, or as with my eating habits, passive resistance.

The only person I knew who went regularly to a synagogue was my grandmother. The best-known *Tempel* was a short walk from her apartment, and occasionally she would take me along. We went upstairs to the women's section and looked down on the sea of black-clad men. The service was entirely in Hebrew, spoken and chanted, partly by the rabbi, partly in the responses by the men. There was no sermon or other part that related to the outside world. The women read along, sometimes mumbling the words, but were not participants. I understood nothing, but nevertheless felt that I was part of what was happening.

Eventually I realized that the words could be translated,

but knowing their meaning only made them more distant. It is one thing to hear them as pure sound and ritual recitation, but once they become understandable, they can be thought about and questioned. There was little that made a positive impression on me.

The formal part of the Jewish religion is, to a large extent, not one of beliefs, but of practices and procedures, the repetition of prescribed blessings, readings, and actions. For the most orthodox they can take up most or even all the available time of daily life. For the rest, the degree of adherence varies all the way to the completely secular.

When I meet another Jew, there is a recognition that we share a common background. Often there is also a common outlook and response to our environment. It is not the religion, or its texts, although there is the shared knowledge of customs and rituals. Quite separately, there is the cultural heritage, and the flow of Jewish history, with its societal contributions. I feel myself enriched by that, and part of it.

* * * * *

The districts outside the Gürtel were suburban and mostly poorer. That's where we lived, in *Hernals*, the 17th district, on its main street, the *Hernalser Hauptstrasse*. Our building was at the corner of a large square, the *Elterleinplatz,* with a worn sign facing the square, "Dr. Bela Lindenfeld, *Haut und Geschlechtskrankheiten*" (skin and venereal diseases). The sign was there throughout my life in Vienna, but I never questioned its meaning, nor did anyone attempt to explain it. *Geschlecht* means "gender." If there was a further meaning, it was, for me, beyond the boundary to the grown-up world.

* * * * *

There were almost no Jews in these districts. I knew only the *Haas* family, who had a tiny grocery store around the corner. Their son, Joshi, was a little older than I. One day I was told, "Joshi no longer has a father." Herr *Haas*' appendicitis was treated too late, the appendix ruptured, and he died.

Infections were common, and there was little defense against them. Minor wounds held the danger of fatal "blood poisoning." Childhood diseases were a constant, dreaded presence. There was frequent mention of whooping cough and measles. I came down with diphtheria and can still feel the difficulty of swallowing, the anxious adults hovering over me, a Professor Hecht called in to treat me, coming at me with what seemed a huge syringe filled with a greenish liquid.

* * * * *

The largest room in the apartment was my father's *Ordinationszimmer*, his office, reception, consultation, and treatment room, only rarely entered by me. It was clean and white, with a *Kachelofen* (coal stove) clad in *Kacheln* (white tiles) in the middle, a couch on the side, and, over the couch, a large spherical metal enclosure that held an ultraviolet lamp. From time to time my father asked me to undress to be under it for about ten minutes to absorb its supposedly healthful radiation. The accompanying danger of skin cancer was not known or considered.

In what I think was an attempt to help my growth and development he would sometimes call me to "Come and get your arsenic!" and put a drop of brownish liquid on a sugar cube for me. I looked forward to it since all I could taste was the sugar. I have occasionally asked physicians about this use of the poison, but none had ever heard of arsenic as an ingredient of a health elixir. One of my friends, a biophysicist, shook his head in disbelief when I told him about it, and said that this treatment is surely the source of my health and longevity.

My father's most prized possession was his microscope, given to him by my mother who was not, however, allowed to touch it. One day he called me to show me the bacteria responsible for syphilis. He was clearly proud of being able to do this, told me what I was looking at, but said nothing about the nature of the disease, and gave me no context or understanding.

* * * * *

Next to my father's room was the narrow waiting room. On one of the long sides was a heavy double sliding door which he would open to admit the patients, on the opposite side a door to the living room. On one of the narrow sides was a window to the street, on the other a door to the hallway and the apartment's entrance. When the bell rang, either the maid or my father answered. There were none of the trappings of the modern industrial-scale medical practice with its receptionist, nurses, accountant, and technicians.

There was just enough space in the waiting room for a couch for the waiting patients that was opened in the evening as a bed for me. I could hear only a little through the door to the living room, but the noise of voices and the knowledge of my parents' presence were a source of comfort.

A door led from the living room to my parents' bedroom. After the remodeling it was part of the tour for visitors. My father would remark about the old-fashioned and undesirable custom of couples sleeping in the same bed.

My mother's bed, slightly wider, was described as the marriage bed. Even though I followed this tour many times, I had no conception of what was meant. Every once in a while, I found my parents together in this bed when I looked for them in the morning, but repressed any thought of what that might imply.

Otherwise, I remember mainly acrimony between them. I suspect that, if it hadn't been for the external dangers and looming disaster, they would have separated. For some months my mother was said to be in a sanatorium. I don't know whether it was a temporary escape or a trial separation.

* * * * *

My father's favorite sibling, and the one with whom he had regular contact, was his sister Ilon, whom I knew from the times when he took me along when he visited his mother. We went by streetcar to the shabby apartment in the *Sobieski-gasse*, not far away, and aunt Ilon answered the door. She had a tiny room where she sewed neckties. My father would say, "*Nu, wie geht's?* (How's it going?) and she would reply, "*Nu, wie kann's einem scho' gehn?*" (How can it go already? i.e., What can you expect?) We then went to the next room, where my grandmother lay in a bed that almost filled the room. We stood at the foot of the bed as she and my father carried on a desultory conversation, mostly about her ailments. After a brief time, my father would take out a banknote and give it to her. She thanked him and we left.

My mother hated the culture of poverty that hung over my father's family, the show of misery, the expectation of handouts. Two family members escaped this environment: my father and Herbert, the son of his sister Irma, both by studying, going to university, and becoming physicians.

My father was born in Budapest in 1882, and around 1900 his mother and he, with Ilon and Irma, moved to Vienna for reasons and under circumstances that I do not know. My father's brother, Karl, or Karoly, continued to live in Hungary. I never met him and I doubt that the brothers were in touch. The only time I heard him mentioned was when my father expressed contempt for his lack of initiative and aspiration to anything more than being a paperhanger.

More about the family came to light recently, when my son-in-law Michael found a professional Viennese genealogist, and, with my children, gave me some hours of the genealogist's time. We learned, contradicting my father's memory and judgement, that Karl retired with a pension from the Hungarian railroad system. He was married twice, and both he and his second wife, Hermin, died in 1956. Their gravestone includes the inscription, in Hungarian, "Here we preserve the memory of their martyred son Laszlo." I know nothing further about the parents or the son.

Karl survived the war, but his sisters Rosa and Ilon were deported to Nazi camps in 1942 and died there, Rosa in Theresienstadt, Ilon in Auschwitz. Was this what happened also to Karl's son?

* * * * *

My father liked to give the impression that that he had been a good student. Late in his life I pursued him with questions about his past and learned that this might not always have been the case. It seems that he had trouble preparing for the Matura, and spent his last high school year in the small provincial town of *Mährisch-Ostrau* (Ostrava). He said that this was so that he would be better able to concentrate on his studies. I suspect that there was also the expectation that he would have an easier time there.

Throughout his life he had nightmares about this exam

and often described the harsh procedures, the obstacles, and the bribes given to the janitor to divulge the names of the chemicals that the students were supposed to analyze. He would talk about the famous professors that conducted the examination, always ending with the triumphal moment when he was not only informed that he had passed, but also given a special commendation.

One of his favorite stories was about his start along a professional path. He had finished the four-year elementary school and wanted to go to high school. Not to the free terminal school, but to the *Gymnasium*, the elite school that led to university entrance, and that required a tuition fee.

His mother made it clear that there was no money for that, and that he should be apprenticed to a tailor or other craftsman, but he said he wanted to go anyway. He set out for the *Piaristengymnasium*, the school of the Piarist fathers, and simply participated. I don't know whether it was after a day, or after a week, but the time came when it was discovered that he had not paid, and he was sent home.

According to this tale, when he was bemoaning his fate after that, there was a commotion at the door as his classmates burst in and emptied a bag of coins on the table, the *Schulgeld*, the money that made it possible for him to stay in school.

Did the charity continue? How did he manage to stay in school for the eight years of its curriculum? There was never any mention of that, or of studies and subjects, of other experiences, or of family members and the life they led. When my father was close to 90 years old, a short time before his death, I stayed in his house with him for about a month. I cooked for him, and we talked. It was a relaxed and comfortable time. I asked him some questions, but not nearly enough. He didn't open up to say more than I already knew. I learned almost nothing more about him or his life. I was reluctant to pry and to bring up subjects that he tried to avoid. The opportunity passed.

Later I asked Herbert, who was fifteen years older than I, about his time in Vienna. He also rejected all questions of family history and said he knew nothing of it. He did not even know the names of all his mother's (and my father's) siblings. I questioned him much more insistently, but again learned almost nothing.

* * * * *

My parents had a circle of friends with whom they got together regularly, mostly in a *Kaffeehaus*, the Viennese coffeehouse, where the waiter would bring you the day's newspaper and you could sit for hours with your coffee and pastry or other food. Occasionally they met in our apartment after I was in bed. The conversation tended to be lightweight with few serious or personal interchanges. There were jokes, which seemed to be primarily on bathroom and sexual themes. Of course, I was not supposed to hear them, but I strained to catch as much as I could from my bed in the adjoining room. I sensed the atmosphere of smoke and conviviality, but could follow or understand little of what was going on. This was to me a mark of the adult world: to be included, to understand, to participate in this kind of talk and banter.

A second feature that seemed to mark adult language was the frequent use of Latin and Greek phrases and proverbs, the heritage of the eight years in the Gymnasium shared by the educated classes. Even casual conversation included a stream of classical references. One that I remember is "*Hic Rhodus, hic salta*," four words that I heard as two. It stuck in my mind and I eventually asked about it: "Here is Rhodes (the Greek island), here jump," meaning loosely, you got here, now do what you said you would do.

These phrases were not seen as ancient or foreign. They were part of the living language. I was sure that after I had learned to use them, a door would open for me. When my speech would include the Latin and the Greek phrases, and when I came to understand the jokes and the sex, that would be it. I would be an adult.

I was often asked what I was going to be when I grew up. More often than not, it was my parents who answered for me, usually suggesting that I was going to be a *Naturforscher,* exploring and studying nature. That meant little to me, although it conjured up the vision of staring at animals in Africa.

There was no doubt that after the four years of elementary school, I would go to a Gymnasium, the kind my parents had gone to, a "humanistic" one with Latin for eight years and Greek for five. There was also another kind, the *Realgymnasium,* where you studied modern languages and a curriculum oriented toward the sciences.

Would it have made a difference if I had had a better understanding of my options? I doubt it. Even though I was not attracted to their profession, my parents were my only role models. I had no idea what a career in science was. Later I made other choices about my education, my jobs, and where I lived, without a good idea of what they implied. Would I make them differently with the knowledge and insight that I have today? There are so many turns, so many crossroads. Who knows how life might have developed with a change in direction, different choices, different mentors?

I went to the nearby Gymnasium of the 18th district for two and a half years. The system of instruction was rigorous, its manner ranged from serious to sadistic. There was no attempt at guidance, no room for choices or any softening of the relentless pace. The teachers of the academic subjects had doctor's degrees and were addressed as *Professor*. When they were not lecturing, they thumbed through the black notebook that had a page for each of us, as they decided whom to call next to answer questions at the blackboard. As they came toward the end of the book, those whose names started with letters near the beginning of the alphabet would relax, while the others tensed.

I remember only one time when I was called out. It was in my third year, when I was twelve years old, in physics class, which was a new subject for us. I liked it, and I liked the teacher, Professor Ungar, with whom I imagined a certain rapport. On this occasion he asked me to describe the working of a gasoline engine. The cycle of intake, compression, explosion, and exhaust, and the operation of the valves fascinated me, even though I knew nothing about cars. I had never been in a car, and I didn't know anyone who had one. But I thought I had the answer down cold. I must have been mistaken. Partway through my presentation the teacher interrupted with "*Setzen. Nicht genügend*" (Sit down, insufficient). It was the failing grade among the four: very good, good, sufficient, insufficient. I slunk back to my seat without ever finding out where I had failed. My grade at the end of the term was a bare pass.

The gasoline engine would be an unlikely subject for a modern physics class, but it was typical for that time. Today it would be regarded as taking the subject away from the underlying physical principles to the less lofty realm of practical applications, away from what is regarded as pure physics to engineering. We may have gained purity, but we have lost the immediacy of dealing with a subject close to experience.

* * * * *

For the first two years, there were three Jews in the class: Tommy Czuczka, George "Schurl" Eisinger and I. We stuck together and became close friends.

Tommy's family lived outside the Gürtel in the working-class apartments that had been called *Karl-Marx Hof* until the right-wing takeover in 1934, and that still showed the holes in the walls from the bullets that were fired at it at that time. Schurl, on the other hand, lived at the edge of the 1st district, in a large and elegant apartment. His father was a physician, like mine, and a *Dozent* at the university, the first step toward becoming a professor and part of the intellectual aristocracy.

About 20 years later, in America, Schurl telephoned and came to visit. He had studied medicine and was now an assistant professor in Philadelphia. During his time with us he did all the talking. He was obsessed with his time in the Gymnasium and its end in 1938. He recited the names of the students in our class in alphabetical order and knew the fate of some of them. He described his nightmares about the ones who had been Nazis with vividly imagined scenes of how they died in battle. He went on to other grisly reminiscences, including one of a time in Egypt that involved keeping body parts of a deceased patient in a bottle of formaldehyde. This was in a Muslim environment where this was strictly forbidden, and where he would have been in serious trouble if he had been found out. Lore was horrified, and after he left, she said she never wanted to see him in the house again.

* * * * *

The alphabetical roll call was such a regular fixture in school that I was not surprised that it had embedded itself in Schurl's mind. It was also an occasion for the expression of the pervasive anti-Semitism. Some of the teachers, as they came to a Jewish name, would pronounce it with an exaggerated emphasis that was meant to show their contempt.

A group of about half a dozen students in the class affected an ostentatiously military manner. Each day, on arrival in the classroom, they greeted each other with formal handshakes and a clicking of heels. They saw themselves as the elite, with a special code of honor. On the day of the Anschluss, when Austria formally became a part of Germany, the handshake was replaced by the until-then forbidden raised-hand salute with a loud *Heil Hitler!*

One day, as I walked to school, I found myself suddenly surrounded by a group of students taunting me. One of them said, "To be short, stupid, and to be a Jew, that's too much," and they started to push me off the sidewalk. As they crowded around me and shoved me, a member of the class's Nazi elite came by. At that time, at any rate, asserting authority was more important than harassment. "*Lost's erm gehn*," he commanded. (Let him go, in the Viennese dialect.) The mob dissolved.

Among the school faculty, the "master race" was most assertively represented by the physical education teachers. They portrayed Jews as smaller, weaker, and less able to participate in sports and physical exercise. They wanted to make us feel that we were a lower form of life, *Untermenschen,* like the *Nibelungen* of the Underworld, best known from Wagner's opera cycle, *The Ring of the Nibelung*.

Before the advent of the Nazis, the most direct and effective challenge to the image of Jews as physically inferior was the establishment of the Jewish sports club *Hakoah*. Renate was a member and competed in swimming. She became the national junior backstroke champion, with a collection of medals and trophies.

I learned to swim in a public pool, suspended from a rope

attached to a belt around my waist while I made frog-like movements. It was not a very efficient system, and all it led to was the tame European breaststroke. That's all I ever saw my parents and my friends do, except for Renate. I admired her enormously, but it was another sign that she lived in a separate and unattainable world. Eventually, as a faculty member, I took a course and learned to swim freestyle, i.e., the Australian crawl. For many years I went to the university's pool every day and swam at least half a mile, and more often a mile. I often thought of Renate and wished she were there. She died during the war, killed by a German bomb in London when she was 23.

* * * * *

Memory is veiled, selective, treacherous. So much of it is kept alive by what others tell us, as we build the legends that are each family's heritage. Some of it lies submerged in darkness to reappear unexpectedly, vividly, after being hidden for years.

A farm in the country. It must have been on a vacation. A girl my age, perhaps three or four. Running after her to a secluded spot behind a barn. Pulling down our pants and exploring the differences between us. Running back. Where were you? No response from me. I knew it was forbidden. From her, to my horror, a shouted answer, *Fuzl zang* (from *zeigen,* to show), hard to follow in their obscure dialect, with its meaning unlikely to be understood by anyone but me. I hadn't heard the dialect words before, and I haven't heard them since, but there was no mistaking them. They remain part of my first memory, real as on the day when I heard them.

I spent my first thirteen years in Vienna, and its images remain vivid in my mind. I see each corner, each building around the large square adjacent to the apartment house where we lived; the street to the east along which I walked during two and a half years to the Gymnasium; the bank; the two streets south toward the center of the city; the side street to the right, up the hill to a church and to my first elementary school. I knew each stone, each detail.

When I saw the square again, decades later, it had not changed. I looked around at the familiar scene, seeing again as reality what for so long had been memory. Suddenly I stopped short. Just off the center was a large fountain. It had been there all the time, of course, and now that I saw it, it took its place again in the remembered tableau. It had not been part of the picture that I had carried with me. The vivid image, so alive, so realistically etched in my mind, had not contained this prominent feature.

* * * * *

I don't think of myself as a Holocaust survivor. I was not deported or detained. I did not suffer. I was carried along by the tide of events. Some of the members of my family died, some that I didn't know, and some that were very close, including my cousin Erika, my grandmother, and members of my father's family, including his sisters Ilon and Rosa. I did not find out about their fates until much later.

My childhood in Vienna, from 1925 to 1938, followed a pattern toward a future that seemed predestined. The four years of elementary school, followed by the beginning years of Gymnasium, represented a program whose outlines seemed to be clear, leading to a professional life that in spirit if not in detail would parallel that of my parents.

I was not a rebel. I tried to do what was expected of me. As a somewhat subdued and introverted only child, I felt secure in my progress along the only path that I knew, toward a time that was unknown, but not unexpected.

EXODUS

My parents were unprepared for what happened. Their life was in Vienna. They had come from what were then other parts of the Austro-Hungarian Empire to its capital. It was a place that you went to, it was not a place that you left. They had no experience of living elsewhere as adults. They didn't travel to other countries for visits or vacations. They came from very different backgrounds, and were very different people. But they had this in common: they built their lives in Vienna, and did not doubt its stability.

Theirs was a heroic generation. They were in mid-career, in familiar surroundings, and thought themselves to be part of a culture that they admired and knew intimately. They had struggled to reach a time in their lives with satisfying work and, in the case of my mother, a career with the promise of continued growth and greater creative possibilities.

Suddenly that life crumbled. After a short time, nothing remained of what they had built. There was no way to know how or where or even whether they would be able to pick up some of the pieces of their existence. Whether to leave, and finding ways to leave, became obsessions. In addition to the bureaucratic obstacles, barely known and changing day by day, there were the personal ones for people like my parents, as they faced changes that they could not comprehend or foresee. Those who were able to leave found themselves moving into unknown territory, where people spoke a different language, with rules of life that were different, seemingly unknowable.

We hear most often about the famous, those who were at the top of their professions and could find sponsors and positions elsewhere. Then there were those who were affluent and had the knowledge and foresight to safeguard assets in other countries.

More often, there were those who were less favored, and who left with only the 10 shillings that they were allowed to take with them. They were forced to adapt to circumstances for which they had no experience, no guiding signposts, and none of the material resources that they had relied on. They found themselves dependent on strangers, in an environment that was often supportive, but could also be hostile.

As time went on there were few failures. The best rose to the top. Many had a strong and sometimes profound influence on their new communities.

I belong to the next generation, to those who had not finished school, and had not established themselves in adult life. It was much easier for us. We were younger, we learned new languages and new ways more easily. Most likely it was also because of the cultural values that had been impressed on us, with their emphasis on education and on work. We were more serious, less carefree than others of our age. We often had early responsibility for other family members. We were rooted in one culture and lived in another, with the opportunity to take from each. At the time the effort to fit in and to adapt dominated all else. It was only later that I realized that we were uniquely favored.

In many ways it is more difficult for those in the generation after us. They are natives. They didn't experience the pressure to adapt to an alien culture, the uncertainties of the transition, or the urgency to succeed. We, their parents, can often help them in material ways that ours could not.

All that would seem to make it easier for them. But the special advantages that we had are not there for them. The knowledge of the previous culture is much attenuated. The early responsibilities and forced seriousness are absent. The legends of the trials and successes of the earlier generations can be intimidating and oppressive. Our presence can be dominating and demanding. We do not always know or understand the very different challenges in our children's lives.

In my case there is also the contentious relationship of my parents. To what extent did that contribute to my own difficulties, and to theirs?

* * * * *

My mother was also a physician. She was fifteen years younger than my father, and by far the more active and imaginative person. While my father was largely passive, she looked for the best schools for me, arranged for extra lessons and activities, and tried to find friends for me. Like my father, she specialized in skin diseases. But in the nature of her work, where she did it, and what she emphasized, she was a world away. Her office was in the apartment where my grandmother lived, right in the center of the city, next to the square with St. Stephen's Cathedral, and across from the home (the *palais*, as it was called) of the archbishop.

Her father had been a banker, but his money disappeared in the hyperinflation following the First World War. After his death a pension remained for my grandmother, who continued to live modestly in their apartment with her maid and companion, Agnes. Apart from the rooms for the two elderly women, there was an entrance hall, my mother's office, and the waiting room that had been the dining room. It held the large table where the Passover dinners took place, and a glass-door bookcase with my mother's cherished books. The spacious rooms and the location of the apartment reflected a former affluence of which little remained. Money was a constant concern for both my parents, never sufficient.

Her sign said *Kosmetik*, which meant primarily the appearance of women's skin. The relation to the patients' self-image led my mother to become more and more interested in psychology. She became a member of the circle of Alfred Adler, the former associate of Freud and founder of the movement he called *Individual Psychology*. This association shaped her professional life and became the foundation of her work. Later, in Canada, her practice was entirely in psychiatry.

A streetcar went from our Hernals apartment to the Ring, and from there it was a short walk to where my grandmother lived and my mother worked. Even while I was still in elementary school, I often walked between the two. Leaving the apartment at Hernalser Hauptstrasse 78, I would cross the Elterleinplatz, past the small street that led uphill to the right to my first school, past the bank at the other end of the square toward the Gürtel, which marked the end of our district. On the way was the public skating rink where I often went in the winter. Once past the Gürtel, the apartment buildings became more imposing.

The street passed the large gray complex of the General Hospital, and widened as it opened to the Ring. I often explored further, especially along the Donaukanal, the branch of the Danube that ran right through the city, while the main part of the river was outside the cosmopolitan area. I became intimately familiar with that part of the city.

* * * * *

Before the Anschluss, the Nazi party had been outlawed. Suddenly, on March 11, 1938, there were swastikas everywhere, as pins on the formerly illegal members and on flags in the streets. I doubt that there were Germans. What you saw were the jubilant Austrians, parading and shouting in unison *Sieg Heil* (hail victory) and other slogans. Later the Austrians liked to portray themselves as victims, but their complicity in what happened and their willing collaboration with the Nazis have been abundantly documented.

Although my mother understood immediately that we had to leave, the rules about who was allowed to leave, and by what means, were never clear. Constantly changing rumors were all there was to go by. In any case, you had to have a country to go to, and you had to have official permission, including a certificate that showed that you owed no taxes, the notorious *Steuerunbedenklichkeitszeugnis*. That meant going from office to office, amassing a long list of stamps and statements that eventually led to this piece of paper. It was valid for one month. After hours in line in a multitude of government buildings, my mother had our certificate and we were ready. Only years later could she bring herself to tell me that the certificate had expired the day before we left without anyone noticing.

When we were about to leave, my mother took one last look at her books, fingering some of her favorites that she didn't expect to see again. The large bookcase with the locked glass doors in my grandmother's apartment had not been accessible to me. As I stood there with her, I saw a small nondescript black Bible with its thin paper. It wasn't much to look at, but a quick scan showed me that it seemed to be complete, including parts that I had not seen before. To my parents' surprise, I had earlier asked for a Bible, and had been given one for my birthday, an elaborate three-volume version with Art Nouveau illustrations. I hadn't let on my disappointment that, impressive as it was, it was not the whole thing. I knew that there were strange, perhaps forbidden parts, and I wanted to see them. The beautifully illustrated excerpts only confirmed that there were secrets that were being kept from me. So now I said, "This is what I've been looking for!" My mother looked incredulous, but took the shabby book and put it in our suitcase, on top of the clothes.

Searching for a safe haven: Our first home in Canada

PART 2: SEARCHING FOR A SAFE HAVEN

TRIESTE

We were going to Trieste, where my mother was born and where members of her family remained. We were going the short distance by plane, because rumor had it that those who tried to leave by train were sent back. At the airport we were about to be searched when the woman who was going to examine us opened the suitcase. The first thing she saw was the Bible. At this show of apparently devout religiosity, she said *Ach Gott*, closed the suitcase, and that was the end of the search. We were on the way. My father remained.

My mother had written to her cousins in Italy, telling them that if we were sent back, she would jump out of the plane. She was a strong-willed woman, and they must have taken her seriously. Family legend has it that everyone else was sent back, while the two of us were taken off the plane as a result of the bribes distributed by the cousins.

We were at the home of Uncle Guido and Aunt Fulvia. The image that has stayed with me is of Uncle Guido at the head of a large table, with other relatives along the sides, as he ceremoniously mixed salad in a large bowl.

My mother had often talked about Trieste. Now she was excited to show me the places of her memories. We walked around a little, but I was feverish and getting more and more ill. It turned out to be tuberculosis.

After the visit to a doctor and some contact with a refugee committee we got on a train to Switzerland. We first went to a small village near Zurich, and the first photograph that I took when we arrived there was of my mother with the Swiss flag flying outside the inn where we stayed. I was very conscious of its symbolism of our new freedom, and the contrast with the repressive atmosphere that we had just escaped. More recently, and perhaps because of that experience, I have resisted the appropriation of the American flag as a symbol of conservative values.

LEYSIN

From there we took the train and then the cogwheel railroad up the mountain to Leysin, in the French part of the country, just east of Lake Geneva. Today it is a town of ski resorts, but at that time it was called *La Cité des Malades*, the City of the Sick, filled with *sanatoria* for people with tuberculosis. Sunshine was the only supposedly curative agent that was known. We were going to the *Sanatorium des Enfants*, the children's sanatorium, which was my home for the next eight months.

In some ways it was a prison for me. We got out only for the occasional *tour du village*, a short walk, two by two, always the same, through the village. The magnificent mountain that dominated the view, the *Dents du Midi*, was inaccessible background. I was not so much alienated as disengaged. The rest of the world seemed no longer to exist.

The beginning was not auspicious. For breakfast we sat at rows of tables in the dining room. The plate of porridge set before everyone looked like vomit to me, and I closed my eyes in nauseated horror. There was no way I would touch it. The staff would have made me eat it in spite of my screams, but my mother was still there and intervened. Was that the right thing to do? Today I don't think so. For the rest of my time there, I was the only one who was not given porridge. My revolt was presumably not just about the porridge. Nevertheless, it was only in recent years that I was able to overcome my revulsion.

There is one other food experience that I remember, and most people find it strange. On the weekends we each got a small piece of cheese after dinner. Saturday it was a tin-foiled triangle of the kind that used to be common here also, and on Sunday it was a piece *of Emmenthaler*, the quintessential "Swiss cheese." I don't know what kind of cheese I had been given at home, but in any case, I had never liked any of it. Here it was, the real thing, and I thought it was great, partly because, and this is the strange part, it was served with jam. To this day I have not met an American who knows cheese with jam as a special treat. In the bleak life of the sanatorium, it was a rare pleasure.

The sanatorium was run by Protestant nuns in traditional habits. They projected an air of severity softened by kindness. *Soeur* (Sister) Rosa was the head. I saw her infrequently, mostly when there was a problem communicating, since, unlike the others, she was from the German-speaking part of Switzerland. Most of my contact was with Soeur Clara, who was young and attractive, and in charge of our floor. There was also a floor with girls. The only time I saw any of them was from a distance, as they were led in single file to the other end of the dining room.

We spent our days on the large veranda, clad in tiny diapers called *caches* (from *cacher*, to hide, because that's what they were supposed to do) so that we could soak up as much of the sun as possible. I had no symptoms and only a vague idea that something was wrong. Some of the boys were much sicker. Each afternoon one of the Sisters came, calling "*Pneumo*!" and a group of boys went with her for a renewal of their pneumothorax, the injection of air to collapse a lung to give it a better chance to heal. There was no other treatment. Streptomycin was discovered at Rutgers University in Selman Waksman's laboratory in 1943, and turned out to be effective against TB. It put the sanatoria devoted to this disease out of business.

* * * * *

I made some friends. One was Maurice, tall, a little older, from the Alsace region of France, near the German border. I recognized that he was drawn to the authoritarian environment in which he grew up. He had plans for a later time. We were joined by Marthe, one of the nurses, a plain girl from the German part of Switzerland. Maurice was the leader, as the three of us plotted to meet in Brazil after the war to found a new community. It was to have some utopian features, mixed with the regimentation that characterized Maurice's outlook. I was excited to be part of a group that thought about the future and that was going to work to shape it. Each of us was lonely, and we were a support group for each other.

It was Maurice who tried to explain sexual intercourse to me. His veiled imagery left me completely bewildered. I was thirteen and must have known something about sex, but whatever it was, I had successfully repressed it to an inaccessible subconscious. There was a certain amount of talk about the subject in the dormitory, but I understood little, and it only added to my confusion.

One likeable and lively boy stayed in bed from one point on. "*Tonton est très malade,*" he is very sick, said Soeur Clara. A short time later he died, and the rest of us were taken to file past his bed for a last good-bye.

It was my first close contact with death. The memory of his being alive a short time earlier, and the confrontation with the dead body combined to create an image that blurred the boundary between reality and illusion.

Since then, I have seen people who were close to me as they died, or shortly before. Others just vanished, ceased to be, with no chance for that last time together, on either side of the divide. When that happened, it added to the loss by leaving the relationship incomplete, suspended, unresolved.

It is common practice to shield children from the reality of death. Sometimes knowledge about their own illnesses is kept from people. Or an attempt is made to remain cheerful, rather than to allow the person to reflect on their life, or on the life of others.

Being together with someone who is very ill and perhaps close to death has often been a positive experience, and part of the healing process for me. It has always been accepted by the person with whom I spent that time. Illness and death are part of life, and we all need to accept that reality.

I don't think I spoke more than a few words of French the whole time I was in Leysin. Maurice and Marthe spoke German, and Soeur Rosa helped when there was a need for official communication. The most important of these came when my mother wrote to ask that I be sent to England to join her. The doctors wrote back that I wasn't ready and needed to stay longer, but she insisted. After their disclaimer of any further responsibility, I was ready to go.

Soeur Clara gave me a French Bible, inscribed "*L'éternel est celui qui te garde.*" (It is the eternal one who watches over you.) It is on my bookshelf, a few feet from where I write. After good-byes, I was once more on my way to the unknown.

THE NEW COUNTRY

My memory of how I got to England is dim. It was spring 1939. It must have been by train and ferry. Plane travel existed, but was not common. I remember only being picked up by a spacious car with a blanket on the seat that had a prominent Star of David woven into the design. I was taken to Tunbridge Wells, a town 30 miles southeast of London, where my mother was now one of two women in charge of a hostel for refugee girls.

The eight months in Switzerland had not been so much difficult as isolating. I was away from my parents, I couldn't speak the language, and I was in an institution with a set pattern to which I had to conform. With the exception of the porridge, I accepted what came my way and tried to do what was expected of me. I don't remember any strong emotions. After thirteen years of an organized and predictable life, everything was strange.

The language was the most immediate barrier. Among my mother's attempts to enhance my education had been French lessons in Vienna. A blind woman came to our home, and made notes for herself in braille by perforating her paper with a stylus. I accepted that without question, and got a start in the language. The stay in Leysin must have helped, even though I didn't speak much there. Now I heard English words for the first time. I understood nothing of the unfamiliar sound. I was disappointed to learn that this was what would be used in our new environment.

At the beginning of my mother's stay in England she had been a household maid, apparently not a very successful one. Once, when the family was out, she wanted to do something special for them and scrubbed the inside of a stained teapot. That was against custom and practice for any teapot, and this one was particularly treasured. When the mistress of the house returned, she was so horrified that she dumped the desecrated piece in the garbage.

I had very little interaction with anyone in the brief time that I was in England. One time I was walking along a street with my mother and her colleague as they talked about their work. I overheard the word *masturbation.* If I had had any inkling what that was, I would have kept quiet. Instead, I asked what it meant. My mother said, "We can talk about that later." Her friend, to her credit, took over and said that it meant playing with yourself. I understood that and was surprised, not so much by the answer as by the fact that it was possible to talk about hidden matters with directness and clarity.

This was a great contrast to the euphemisms, the veiled references, and the practice of hiding reality from children that had been characteristic of my earlier experiences. It took a long time to absorb this lesson and to free myself from obscurantism, to become direct myself, and to avoid silence and evasion.

My mother had asked for me to join her because she had received our permit to go to Canada. I had an Austrian passport, which showed that I had been given permission to enter Switzerland and that I had been in Leysin. She was convinced that we would be denied entry if the authorities knew that I was there for treatment of tuberculosis and was equally sure that the name Leysin would immediately give that away. She did the unthinkable and altered the passport: She carefully crossed out Leysin, and wrote in *Lausanne* instead.

We boarded the *Duchess of Atholl* in Southampton for our weeklong voyage to Montreal. We had access to only a small piece of outside deck, and I was seasick on all but the first and last days.

On the way my mother looked at a map to get some idea of where we were going. In Vienna she had been a member of a feminist group. This was in the 1930s, when attention to women's rights was a lot less common than it is now. One of her friends was A. H. (for Anna Helene) Aszkanazy, known as *Aha*. She got out of Austria with her two daughters within a day of the Anschluss, but her husband was arrested and died in police custody. Unlike others we knew, she had money outside the country. She looked for a place to go to and found the village of Sooke, on Vancouver Island, off the coast of British Columbia. This is where we were heading.

A group of Yiddish-speaking Jews from Eastern Europe were on board. It was the first time that I heard the language, which I took to be a distorted form of German. One of them quizzed me about my family, making an effort to use words that I would understand. He asked whether we had a house or a car, and eventually turned to the others, shrugged his shoulders, and reported to them that we were not rich. "*E arme Doctor,*" (A poor doctor) was his conclusion.

It was raining on the day we first saw land, and when we got closer, there was a rainbow, traditionally seen as a good omen. The ship docked, and we climbed the stairs to the railroad station. We settled on the black patent leather coach seats for our journey of four days and four nights to the west coast.

Along the way, a family with a boy about my age joined us in our compartment. We couldn't really communicate, but he showed me his comic books. I had no idea what they said or represented, but they were my first introduction to the new culture.

In Vancouver, we wasted no time getting on the boat to Victoria, where we were picked up and driven to the place that would be our home for the next months.

SOOKE

How on earth did we get to this isolated farmhouse? To us city dwellers it seemed to be at the edge of the known world. Immigration to Canada was severely restricted, but Aha made it possible for about a dozen of us to join her "family" at Sooke Harbour House in the tiny village of Sooke as farmers. A more unlikely group of farmers is hard to imagine. We were Jews, Catholics, and political refugees, a miscellaneous collection of people who had known only city life in Vienna. Now we were rootless, with no picture of where we were or where we were going. Aha's generosity and enterprise gave us a new start.

There were no visible neighbors. It was 24 miles from the provincial capital, Victoria, which was accessible by car, but inaccessible to me. My only memory is of the farm. It included a room where guests were served coffee, tea, and Viennese pastries, and a display of handicrafts. I don't know how people heard about it, but some came. In Leysin I had learned to make leather wallets and cigarette cases as a way to occupy time, and as a future activity for those who would be too disabled for more active work. Now I was happy to be able to make them as my contribution.

They were sold to guests and given away to supporters.

It was obvious enough how the system worked, but no one explained the cooperative nature of the enterprise to me. I remember being disappointed that I had no say in what happened to my work and that it was dealt with without my being asked or told. Later I saw many times how essential it is to be clear about expectations, to be told and to understand one's role and obligations, and to know what is permitted and what is not.

My knowledge of English did not progress very much since everyone spoke German. Another obstacle was that I was sick for part of the summer. I developed pleurisy, which led to some I-told-you-so letters from the Leysin sanatorium, whose doctors had advised that I wasn't ready to leave. I don't know whether they were right, but I got over the illness in a few weeks and had no further problems.

I saw myself as my mother's companion, and she generally shared her thoughts with me. When there were letters addressed to her, I opened and read them until she told me that I wasn't allowed to do that. I was hurt, but also understood, and, in fact, was relieved to be in a more appropriate place in relation to her.

Aha's feminism was militant, and she made it clear that she considered males, in general, to be inferior to females. She often mentioned Robert Briffault, the author of *The Mothers*, a book that describes a society where women were the dominant gender. Some of it was apparently written in her house, and it clearly had a great influence on her.

Aha's two daughters were about the ages of my cousins Renate and Erika. The older one, Lisl, was gentle and soft; Lore, the younger one, a driving replica of her mother. Just as had been true for my cousins, I saw them as much closer than I was to the adult world. They were protective of me, and I admired them and was very fond of them.

The atmosphere in the house tended to be highly charged, with a lot of talk at the table, much of it about politics and some about sex. I tried to follow what was being said, but mostly felt left out. Eighteen-year-old Lore described her crushes, including one on the Prince of Wales, later King Edward VIII and Duke of Windsor. Looking back, I can see that her eventual husband bore a striking physical resemblance to him.

The first native English speakers that I knew were Mr. and Mrs. Yendall, the couple whom Aha hired to cook, do chores, and drive her car, with its jump seats, large enough for about eight. I remember almost nothing of the other members of the group. I have a visual memory of some, but remember none of their names. At the end of summer, everyone began to make new plans. My mother moved with me to Vancouver, to begin yet another new life.

VANCOUVER

Aha and my mother were strong links for each other to the life they both had known in Vienna. They had the kind of intimacy that comes with long-shared experience, and they cherished the strong bond between them. They saw each other frequently, until one evening, when both were invited for a social evening to the house of a mutual acquaintance. The discussion turned, as it usually did, to politics. The hostess defended Stalin's regime in the communist Soviet Union. The volatile Aha declared that this was just like defending Nazism, and that she could not remain in a house where this was tolerated. She not only got up and left, but expected my mother to follow her. My mother was not given to public outbursts and remained. Aha announced that she would never speak to her again, and indeed, she never did.

Their strong friendship had helped sustain them in an environment that to some extent would remain alien to both. Over an abstract principle that had no bearing on their lives, they lost the support that only they could give each other. A number of people tried to bring about a reconciliation, but without success.

I knew the concept of being *beleidigt* (offended), not uncommon in my parents' circle. It was a state of mind, the response to a real or imagined slight, assuming malicious intent in infractions of the accepted code when it was often not intended. Not speaking to each other, usually for some limited time, was a frequent outcome. I know no other example where the rupture was so inflexibly permanent.

My mother and Aha had many friends and acquaintances, but none could replace the closeness that they had shared. It was a sad example of a rigidity that I was familiar with, and that I associated with their generation and their European origin.

* * * * *

In Vancouver my mother found a small apartment in a building right in the commercial center of the city, trying to recapture what she had known in Vienna. There was just enough room for her work, and for the two of us to live.

Throughout our travels she had carried a small *electrolysis* machine for removing hairs one at a time. It was specially built for her by a colleague, and she said it did the job better than any commercially available device. She now set up shop, removing unwanted hair for women. Her eyesight was bad, but she hunched over her clients day after day, squinting at them through the strong lenses of her glasses.

The apartment was right at one of the busiest corners of the city. There was a traffic light, and every time it changed from green to yellow, from yellow to red, and so on, a loud bell rang. It was not a residential neighborhood, and no one thought of complaining. Except my mother. She called city hall and, presumably after wrestling with others, got to talk to the mayor. That's remarkable, even though Vancouver was much smaller than it is now. The mayor, Lyle Telford, was a physician, so that there was a bond between them. After some back-and-forth, the bell got turned off, and she and the mayor remained on friendly terms and saw each other socially from time to time.

He was a member of what was then called the CCF party (Canadian Commonwealth Federation), the reform-minded progressive party which was strong in Vancouver and in British Columbia. I don't know whether it was through him, but she got to know others in the party as well.

Strangely, she also had a connection to his rival, the sometime-mayor Gerry McGeer, from the more conservative Liberal party. His niece, Mary, was a social worker and member of the social work faculty at the University of British Columbia (UBC). She became a close friend to my mother and later to me. She did not share her uncle's, and later her brother's, conservative political leanings. After her marriage, she would say "I'm glad my name isn't McGeer."

Naturally, my mother wanted to regain her physician's license. The local medical society ruled that she would have to spend a year at a Canadian medical school before she would be allowed to take the required examination. My father, several years later, was not subjected to this hurdle. In fact, I never heard of anyone else who had this prerequisite imposed. Was it because she was a woman? Or because she was the first refugee in the area to seek to reestablish herself in the medical profession?

One day she got a call from an acquaintance, asking whether she would see a patient, at night and in secret. She agreed, and a man was ushered in late one evening. The eczema on his anus had resisted the attentions of various doctors. She gave him an ointment and he was cured.

It turned out that he was a leading politician in the neighboring province of Alberta. A week later, a letter arrived from the Alberta medical society, with a certificate granting the permission that she had been denied in British Columbia to take the examination of the Medical Council of Canada. She looked at it and thought about it for a long time. "I don't want to move to Alberta," she said, "and I will never be able to practice here if they find out that I did not follow their rule." The piece of paper that she desperately wanted was put aside.

After two years of work, her savings were still insufficient to allow her to spend a year away. She contacted Vancouver's Jewish community and asked for a loan. This was a group primarily of people who had come near the end of the 19th century, at the time of pogroms and persecutions in Eastern Europe. They knew that the secular and intellectual Jews newly arrived from central Europe were not likely to be their friends. The division was just as I had seen it in Vienna: On one side were the religious and traditional Jews, often brought up in Yiddish-speaking households; on the other, the assimilated Jews, who had made every effort to behave and become like the dominant group, speaking German in Austria and Germany, and English in Canada. For my parents, the adherence to orthodox observances and old traditions represented a return to customs that they wanted to escape.

My mother got the loan and left for the nearest medical school at the University of Manitoba in Winnipeg, half a continent away. It took enormous determination, but she saw no other choice. I stayed in Vancouver, so what I say about her time away is inferred, indirect information.

Unexpectedly, it turned out to be a good year for her. For the first time in many years, she was free of all family responsibilities. My father was not part of her life, and I was taking care of myself in Vancouver. The young students looked up to her, and she loved being surrounded by them and taking them under her wing. There were even hints of a friendship with a (male) faculty member.

At the end of the year, she took the exam and failed. It was twenty years since she had been a student. She had to use a language she was still learning. The methods and the culture were unfamiliar to her. It is not surprising that the obstacles were too great. Still, she was not a person to give up. She stayed in Manitoba, and although she could not practice medicine independently, she was given permission to take a temporary job in a psychiatric facility. She did not return to Vancouver until she passed the exam on the third try, a year later.

A mixed education: First grade class, Vienna

PART 3: A MIXED EDUCATION

HIGH SCHOOL

In the fall of 1939, after we moved to Vancouver, I started grade nine in King George High School. In Vienna I had finished the four years of elementary school, and two and a half years of Gymnasium, with close to nothing after the Anschluss and the following year in the sanatorium. I was given credit for that time anyway.

At first, I understood nothing of what was going on. Everyone was kind, but I was lost in a land of incomprehensible language and customs. I sat in the first row but could not follow what the teacher or anyone else said. The forced total immersion was effective, and it didn't take long for me to begin to understand and participate. The school in Vienna may have been brutal and hostile, but its academic level was much more advanced. Most of the subject matter was easy for me, and the language followed. After a few months I was functioning.

Miss Creelman was the English teacher. I can't begin to say how much I learned from her. She belonged to the prescriptive school. The way you said something was either right or wrong. Years later I saw the announcement of her death. I was sad as I thought of her and that I never told her how much she had influenced me. I still try to make sure that my pronouns have antecedents, that my participles are not dangling, and that my infinitives are not split. The Latin class was a lot easier than what I had already been through in Vienna. To my surprise, even in this introductory class we read from an original text (was it *Julius Caesar*?), rather than endlessly repeating the grammar drills that were all that Latin had meant to me before.

The school was in an old building close to the bridge that separated the downtown area from residential sections. When I looked for the school on a later visit to Vancouver, I discovered that a second building had been added. Later still, both were taken down to make way for the expansion of the commercial area of the city that by that time was a far cry from the minor outpost it had been when we first saw it.

For my classmates, I must have been a curiosity. For me, they were the aliens. I wanted to be one of them, but didn't know how. I didn't understand their easy banter and barely knew how to talk to them. Eventually there was a girl I liked. Talking with Jean didn't seem that hard, and after a while I asked her to go to a movie with me. I picked her up at her house, where I met her father, who seemed to accept my presence well enough. We went out several times, and I remember her telling me that I should walk protectively between her and the street. I fantasized about her, but we didn't go beyond holding hands. One time she said, "I'm in a good mood today." I thought that might be an invitation and was paralyzed. The moment passed. On another occasion, a year later, when we were no longer classmates, I tried to put my arms around her. She drew back and said, "I already have a boyfriend." I didn't know what to say and there was only awkwardness. I didn't see her again.

In the summer, Joe Kania arranged for me to go to a YMCA camp. He was a non-Jewish immigrant who had come from

Austria in 1913. He had worked after high school, gone to UBC, and later to MIT for a PhD in Geology. Now he was with a large financial and investment firm. He talked about himself as a self-made man and advocated working as he had done and becoming independent before going to college.

The camp was my introduction to an outdoor life that was entirely new to me. I tried to do whatever the other boys did, but was clearly an outsider. Mary McGeer's two brothers, Pat and Pete, a little older than I, were counselors. I liked and admired them, but when they talked, it was hard for me to follow. They knew about building things and talked confidently about two-by-fours, different kinds of wood, and tools that I had never seen. It wasn't just that they knew things that I didn't know. It seemed to me that they knew things I would never know. Again, I was in alien, incomprehensible territory.

* * * * *

When school started again, I found that I had been skipped ahead two years to grade twelve. I don't know what I missed, but had no trouble keeping up. The remnants of my education in the Austrian Gymnasium seemed to be enough to keep me going. I was more confident, but there were huge gaps. One was my social awkwardness, now accentuated by my being two years younger than my classmates. I'm not sure that I felt any more awkward than I had the previous year. One reason is that there was not the sexualized atmosphere that I see for that age group today. Was it there and I was just not sensitive to it? I don't think so. My memory is that studying was taken seriously. I had some friends I saw occasionally after school. The only dance was at the end of that year. My mother urged me to ask a girl to go with me, and suggested one whom I barely knew and didn't find attractive. I reluctantly followed her advice, even though I didn't know how to dance, and we shuffled along for a while.

The school part again came quite easily for me. I had been told to raise my hand and ask if there was something I didn't understand. I remember only one time when I did that. It was in English class near the beginning of the year. To illustrate some grammatical point, the teacher told us to write down "Jack and Jill went up the hill to fetch a pail of water." I put up my hand and said, "Can you tell me what a pail is?" The teacher didn't know me and looked nonplussed. After a moment of silence, the class burst out laughing. I was confused and embarrassed, but not particularly traumatized, because the atmosphere in general had been kind and supportive.

At the end of the school year there was a contest to write something for the yearbook, and my mother urged me to enter. I thought that was far-fetched, but put together something not very original that I called "Fables my mother told me." I won. I was pleased, but also astonished and embarrassed, because I didn't think I deserved this prize. The reward was a copy of the yearbook. I had it up to a couple of years ago, but now I don't know what happened to it.

GETTING TO WORK

If there was a graduation ceremony, I don't remember it. All I knew was that I wanted to work. A man in the building where we lived told me about a lampshade factory that he had some connection to, and I started there on my first free day. The work consisted of cutting wire by stepping on a foot pedal, to lengths given by the distance between two nails. It was repetitive, mind-numbing work. When I woke up in the middle of the night after my first day, my foot was still stepping on an imaginary pedal. On the next day a variation was to cut thinner wire, this time with a hand-operated lever.

After my first full week I was looking forward to getting my promised pay of eight dollars, and was quite upset to get an envelope with seven one-dollar bills and 33 cents in change. I was told that the full amount would have been for a 48-hour week, but was less because the factory was now on a 44-hour schedule. After a short time, another opportunity arose and I moved on.

I was now an office boy with a salary of 35 dollars a month for the Canadian Credit Men's Trust Association. I fetched, carried, copied, filed and stacked. I was intent on doing what was expected of me in what was once more a strange environment. No one told me what was being done there (it was a credit-rating agency), that the information being handled was confidential, or that it was not OK to take pencils home.

A supposed bonus was a reduced-fare pass for the bus and streetcar system, but I thought I could do better by using a bicycle. The only problem was that I didn't have one. My mother suggested that I ask an acquaintance, a fellow refugee, for a loan. I called her and she agreed to lend me the cost of the bike, 50 dollars, to be repaid at the rate of five dollars per month.

This was the first of three such jobs that I had during the year. The second one (at 45 dollars a month) was in the Marine Building, then the tallest commercial building in Vancouver, now barely visible among its giant neighbors. One of my duties was to take over for the woman who normally handled the telephone when she went out for lunch. That meant answering the phone and plugging a patch cord into the proper slot. The place for the boss on the top floor lit up red when he picked up his phone. He was a famous and shadowy figure, and I had no idea what he did. One day I connected him but then did not withdraw my own cord. After a moment, he bellowed, "Cut yourself off, operator!"

The third job, for still a little more money, was with the Japanese Fishing Vessels Disposal Committee. It was 1942, during the Second World War. There had been Japanese and Chinese students in my school classes. They all spoke perfect English. Their parents had lived in Canada since the beginning of the century or longer. The Chinese population was most visible in their family-run grocery stores. The Japanese dominated the extensive fishing industry. Now that Japan was the enemy, the government decided, as in the United States, that they were a danger and a threat. They were forced to sell their boats.

Each boat was described in a sale document signed by the

members of the Committee overseeing the sales. One of my tasks was to take the papers to the Japanese member of the Committee in the part of town where most of the Japanese lived, and watch as this sad-faced man added his signature.

Did this remind me of the crimes and humiliations that I had been witness to? The old Jewish men forced to bend to the ground to scrub the pavement? The expropriations of businesses? Leaving the apartment where we lived, and seeing it and all we had, taken over by others? And all that was worse? At the earlier time, I watched and experienced what was happening as if it were happening on the other side of a screen, making it seem remote, barely touching me. Here again, I saw events as through a veil. This time I was a participant. Did I share the guilt?

The expropriation of the fishing boats was made by law. I had seen and lived with governmental decrees and considered them to be final and immutable. It wasn't until much later that I learned it was possible to protest and oppose them.

Today there are millions of "undocumented" immigrants. That concept didn't exist for the wave of immigrants of which I was a part. If you were in a country not your own, you had to have "papers." You could only come to the United States if you had an Affidavit of Support, a guarantee that someone would back you up financially if ever you couldn't take care of yourself. There was no possibility, as far as we knew, of being here illegally. Governmental edicts were unassailable, immutable. It took a long time to learn that this need not always be so.

* * * * *

Partway through the year my father arrived. I was seventeen and hadn't seen him since we left Vienna four years earlier.

He had stayed behind when my mother and I left Vienna. Like so many, he didn't believe that the madness could last. Two weeks after we left, he was arrested by the police, and after a short time he was taken to Buchenwald, one of the notorious concentration camps that so many did not survive. He never talked about his time there. I don't know what it was like to live there or what it took to get out. At the time, the war was still over a year away and, at least for some people, it was possible to get out if they had a country to go to. Visas to the United States were restricted by a quota system, and most other countries shut off all access.

The one place where no visa was required was Shanghai. You had to have a ticket to go there, and I remember that it cost 50 English pounds. This was an impossible amount of money for my mother, but she found someone who put it up, and this is how my father got out of the camp, out of Germany, and survived. He didn't go to Shanghai, but followed in our footsteps to Italy where, he said, in his sometimes-theatrical way, he threw his ticket into the ocean. He went on to England, where he was promptly interned as an "enemy alien." For us, the difference between a Jewish refugee and a Nazi was laughably obvious, but that was not so for the British authorities. Again, I never heard a word from him about what it was like to be a prisoner. You could apply to be sent overseas, which he did, thinking that he would be sent to Canada, where we were by that time. Instead, he was sent to Australia.

Permission to enter Canada reached him, but was canceled when the authorities found that he was now an enemy alien. When it was eventually restored, my mother was at the medical school in Winnipeg, and only I was there to welcome him when his ship docked in Vancouver.

There was no particular show of emotion on my part.

There was more by him. I was focused on what I needed to do, and just tried to deal with the tasks at hand. There were only the two of us and I was in charge. I knew my way around, I wanted to show him where he was, and I was going to take care of him. We must have talked quite a lot, but I remember no in-depth discussions. Just as he never talked about his experiences as a prisoner, he didn't talk about his early life or his family. There were a few anecdotes, rehearsed set pieces, like the one about his school money, but I remember nothing that opened him up and revealed his inner life. We lived side by side, but I can't say I got to know him more than superficially.

When my mother left for medical school, Joe Kania and his wife invited me to stay in their house, where I had a tiny room, really more like a closet, when my father arrived. Mrs. Kania didn't want me to feel that I was getting charity, and asked me to pay six dollars a month. They had two small children, and I was aware that she was concerned that I behave "properly," especially with the little girl. I think I did, but I thought the atmosphere was somewhat uptight, and was not sorry to leave.

My father and I moved to a room where the rent was fifteen dollars a month. I don't know how that was paid. All other expenses came out of what I earned, and I was proud to be the only wage earner in the family.

At some point he asked me to call him by his first name, rather than the childish "Papa," and I gradually got used to calling him Bela. He received permission to take the medical exam without the obstacles that had been put in my mother's way. He studied, and on the third try he, too, passed and set up a practice. He was now more than 60 years old.

WINNIPEG

The following year, 1943, I received a government loan to attend the University of Manitoba in Winnipeg, where I enrolled to study chemical engineering, which looked to be a pretty sure bet to lead to a job on graduation. Social sciences or humanities were not real options. There was no way I knew that would lead to employment in these fields, and studying them seemed frivolous. On the other hand, working with different materials, learning to manipulate and use them, was attractive to me. I took the train to Winnipeg and found a room downtown near the university in Mrs. McEachern's boarding house where I paid 27 dollars a month for room and board.

I could more easily have remained in Vancouver and gone to the University of British Columbia. I can't tell what made me go to Winnipeg. Presumably I thought I would be near my mother. She had finished her year of medical school and was preparing to retake the exam that she had failed. She was working in a mental hospital in Brandon, 130 miles away, and I took the train to visit her just once during that year.

The previous year, while I was working in Vancouver, I had taken correspondence courses and exams that led to credit for what was called "grade thirteen," equivalent to the first year of college. I took German and French, which took almost no work on my part. Chemistry was easy enough, but required a laboratory component. I bought chemicals at the drugstore, followed the instructions in the kitchen, and submitted lab reports. I looked into doing the same for physics, and saw that it would be quite impossible for me to get the necessary equipment. I took the exam, but didn't submit the notebook that would show that I had done the experiments. No one ever noticed this omission, and it didn't seem to affect my subsequent career.

The engineering curriculum was considered to be an elite course of study that took five years, a year more than other bachelor's degrees. Its higher status was reflected in the cost of tuition, which I remember as $225, compared to $175 for the "arts" students.

My year of grade thirteen led me to enroll in the second year of engineering, eager to move ahead, and unhappy that I was made to take another introductory physics course. I thought I knew all I needed to know about that, found it boring, didn't pay much attention, and didn't do particularly well. My impression was that there was "physics," which I liked, and something called "elementary physics," a mixture of topics that didn't seem to have anything to do with each other. That view stayed with me. Later, when I taught this kind of course myself, I restructured it to meet my criticisms, and eventually wrote a textbook for it.

I felt quite differently about the math course. It included my first exposure to calculus. I was excited to see how a change in one quantity could affect changes in another, and that there were tools to understand the relationships. Professor Lawson was an excellent teacher and a very appealing person. He described the subject and the required mathematical manipulations clearly and convincingly. My admiration for him rose even more when I learned that he wrote for the university's literary journal.

* * * * *

I can't tell you what else I may have learned, because the rest of the year was a blur dominated by meeting my first serious girlfriend.

I don't remember where I met Seemah. Probably at a meeting of a Jewish group. She was a member of Habonim, a labor Zionist organization. She had a boyfriend there, and it didn't take long for me to want to take her away from him. I don't know how that happened, but it did. I was eighteen and she was a high school student of about the same age. I was again trying to cope with a new environment and new tasks. There was little room for thought of responsibilities beyond the present.

She wanted to be an actress, and I saw her perform just once. It was a monologue of which I understood nothing because it was in Yiddish. But the lilt of her speech and her radiance are vivid to me still. We spent a lot of time together during that year and became close. The physical attraction was strong, but we were scared to death of the possibility of a pregnancy, which we knew we couldn't handle. Birth control was presumably available, but we knew nothing about how to get it or how to use it. We touched and fondled, but agreed to stay away from actual sex. Was that an indication of maturity or immaturity? Perhaps some of each.

Through Seemah, I became familiar with the Winnipeg Jewish community. Her father was the head of the orphanage. Her family, the Wilders, and the others I came to know, were descendants of Yiddish-speaking immigrants from Eastern Europe who had come in the 19th century. The Wilders, the Bermans, the Zipurskys, and the others were a close-knit group. They had struggled and had made it to the middle class. Their contact with non-Jews seemed to be on an "as needed" basis. They took care of each other, and they adopted me. When summer came, Mrs. Zipursky asked me to stay at her family's house.

No wonder that I think fondly of my time in Winnipeg. The good feelings had an additional origin in the inhospitable climate, which seemed to draw people together. I remember walking along the street in the winter, ducking from one doorway to the next, stopping in each to warm my ears so they wouldn't freeze. In the summer it got blazingly hot.

The rest of the physical environment was not helpful. Winnipeg is the capital of Manitoba, one of Canada's three prairie provinces, all of them flat, with few cities. The fields stretch as far as the eye can see.

When classes were over, I found a job in a creamery for 40 cents an hour. Milk was delivered in large cans in the morning and made into butter. We wore rubber shoes since the floor was perpetually wet, covered with the residue that overflowed from the large tanks. One part of the work was to get into the tanks to scrub them. "Milkstone is tough," was the comment of the supervisor. Still, I was glad I didn't have my classmate Zalman's assignment. He had to taste a spoonful of milk from each can as it came in, grade it, and then spit it out. An occasional particularly unpleasant grade was called "metallic." He tasted so much milk all day that later, at home, his spit continued to be white.

After a while I found another job. It was at the same rate of pay, but seemed to have some advantages. I had to assemble containers to hold coal for residential furnaces. Repairmen were sent out to service the furnaces, and I went along as a helper. I would head for the coal stoker, a large screw controlled by a thermostat, that propelled the coal to the furnace. My job was to remove the coal so that the rest could be cleaned. I remember one house where I was in the basement with a small window above my head, through which I had to shovel out the coal. With each shovelful, half of it would fall back on my head.

Earlier I had applied for still another job, one I really wanted. It was with the municipality, as a flagman on street construction. I was told that they would let me know when there was an opening. I kept calling, and one day they said yes, come on in. When I showed up, they found out that I was not a Canadian citizen, and said I couldn't have the job. I kept the coal job, but was not very good at it, and less than attentive. One day I was called in and fired.

While I was in Winnipeg, my father was in Vancouver, studying for his exam. He couldn't practice, but, like my mother, he could take temporary jobs. That summer, he was in Ocean Falls, a town along the coast of British Columbia. I had just started the first of my menial jobs when he wrote to tell me that, as a result of his efforts, I could come to work in the paper mill there for 200 dollars a month. It was more money than I was making, and promised to be interesting, but I said no. I wasn't going to leave Seemah.

Was that a wise decision? Could I have stayed in touch with Seemah and seen her again later? It could have been a turning point in my life, both in my relationship with her and in my pursuit of a profession. I'll never know. I lived in the moment and could not see beyond it. I did not think of other plans or of another time.

I had just one last job in Manitoba. Close to the end of summer, a call went out for college students to help with the harvest. It paid three dollars a day plus room and board. As the wheat was cut, it was bundled into sheaves by a machine, and we city kids were to pick them up one at a time with a pitchfork and throw them on top of the growing pile on the hay wagon. The outcome was predictable. The wagons were piled high, the sheaves were heavy, and I just wasn't strong enough. After three days, the farmer took me aside and said that both of us would be better off if I quit. I took the train back and arrived, still covered with hay, in the middle of the night at Mrs. Zipursky's, who didn't know whether to laugh or cry. I was out of money and out of options and had to go back to Vancouver.

* * * * *

That's not quite the end of the story. Later in the fall, Seemah wrote to say she would be in Vancouver. How did she manage that? Did she come just to see me? I don't know. One day my parents were away and we went to bed together. We fumbled and stumbled and it didn't work very well. I was mortified at having failed.

What would have happened if we had given ourselves a little more time? If we could have relaxed a little? If I hadn't taken it as now or never? She left soon after, and I did not see her again.

I could have followed up. Her brother lived near Vancouver. Her sister was married to a physicist who was at Los Alamos at the time. This was the first time I heard about a laboratory and a city that were so secret that even the family couldn't know about them. Later, I thought I might be able to find him at some meeting and ask about Seemah, but the occasion never came.

More fundamentally, I was scared of a closer relationship. I loved her, but I wasn't ready for more. I didn't know how to think of a future, or to make plans for it. Perhaps I had too much of my father's passivity and not enough of my mother's active engagement.

UBC

It was time to register at the University of British Columbia. I expected to use the same government loan program as the previous year, but was told that it was not available. Instead, I was going to get some money outright, but only half of what I needed for tuition. My holdings were at zero and it looked as if I could not continue. At that point I was interviewed by Walter Gage, a professor of mathematics. He knew just about everyone on campus and was probably the best-liked person there. He later became a dean, and eventually the president of the university. He said he would see what he could do, and came up with the rest of what I needed.

For the engineers, the curriculum was completely prescribed, without electives. I remember several courses that I enjoyed that year. Gage was the math professor with more calculus, and I liked him, as everyone did. There was physics with Mr. Spence, who singled me out to take over a class session for a demonstration. I set up an experiment on an electrical phenomenon that I don't remember, except that I had to connect a lot of wires. The experience encouraged me to change my plans from chemical to electrical engineering.

A course I wouldn't have chosen was geology, but it turned out to have a lasting impact on me. Mining is an important industry in British Columbia, and the course was taught by experienced professionals. There were four professors. Three gave lectures: one on structural geology, one on rocks, and the third on fossils. But what I liked best was the mineralogy lab with the fourth professor, Harry Warren. At the first meeting, he talked about engagement rings, with the message that there were many more interesting possibilities than diamonds. Minerals came alive in his class, and an interest in them has remained with me.

By this time my parents had opened offices and begun to earn money. Since my mother's return from Manitoba, we lived in a small apartment, and after some time my parents bought a house. It needed some renovations, and they said I could suggest something. That's when I asked for a darkroom in the basement.

I already had a camera in Vienna, and I remember posing my mother for a photograph as she walked along a tree-lined boulevard. Now I could process my own pictures, especially after an acquaintance of my parents lent me an enlarger. I say lent, but she never asked for it back. I became quite skilled, and photography was a part of my life from then on. What I liked best was to photograph people at moments that were characteristic for them. I like that it's visual and art-related, and it contrasts with my other activities. I've had my work in a few shows, and once won a local award.

* * * * *

The first apartment, the one with my mother's office, was in the heart of the downtown shopping area, no longer recognizable in the metropolis that Vancouver has become. A second apartment was also in that area, nearer the harbor, with its spectacular views of the mountains.

The eventual house was in an attractive tree-lined residential neighborhood. It was a desirable area then, but not with today's prices that shuts it off from all but quite wealthy people. It took over an hour by streetcar and bus to get to the university. That was my daily commute for the five years that I was at UBC.

I was conscious of the physical beauty of my surroundings. The mountains to the north were a constant presence. They rise close to the water of the harbor, in a harmony that changes as the light changes, and at the same time remains the same in its outline. In the distance beyond, the farther and larger snow-capped peaks can often be seen, and add a feeling of unending depth and mystery.

Even as I never tired of what I saw, I felt that I was far from the center of the world. Whatever was significant seemed to happen elsewhere, as did the essential decisions that determined the political structure. The United States border was not far away, but I was a "stateless" person and could not cross it. I liked where I was, but also felt trapped, far from the more exciting life that I imagined elsewhere.

I eventually became a Canadian citizen and was by then very familiar with the local political scene. I looked forward to being able to vote, and I was disappointed to learn that to participate in a municipal election you had to be a property owner. I didn't get to vote until I became a United States citizen more than a decade later.

Politics has been part of my life almost as far back as I can remember, helped along by my parents' interests and by the turmoil of the time. In the earliest instance, I remember my father talking to an acquaintance who asked what future he saw for me. He answered that he hoped "*dass er ein guter Sozialdemokrat wird*" ("that I would become a good Social Democrat"). There is no counterpart in the United States. The nearest is probably the liberal wing of the Democratic party, and that is where I find my allegiance. The party was strong in Vienna, but it was usually overwhelmed in the rest of the country by the conservative Catholic party.

* * * * *

What did I learn during my time at UBC? In my supposed specialty, not so much. Electrical engineering was all about machines: motors, generators, transformers. I wrote a paper on oil circuit breakers. Computers and transistors didn't exist. Electronics was the only modern course, and I learned about diodes, triodes, and pentodes (at that time all glass tubes several inches high) and how they can be connected to construct amplifiers and oscillators. The department was run benignly by Hector McLeod, who later became Dean of Engineering. The present building of the electrical engineering department is named after him and has his portrait at the entrance.

Afternoons were taken up by labs, mostly cook-book, make-work, time-eating. My criticism goes further than that. The courses were strictly for the transmission of information, such as one might get from a book, and often not that clear. In a course in surveying, my grade was 50 percent, the lowest passing grade, the closest I ever got to failing.

Some weeks of actual surveying followed, eating into the time available for a summer job. Classes were lectures with little attempt at interaction. The curriculum of the last two years was largely in the chosen specialty, narrow in extent, as well as in the way the subjects were treated. I didn't learn much about what I now know to be important. There was hardly anything about electric and magnetic fields and the way they behave and relate to the observed effects. I envied my friends who had more interesting activities. I would have liked to take courses with some of the well-known teachers of literature, history, and economics.

* * * * *

Extracurricular activities provided me with a wider community. I joined the International Relations Club and was elected president of the Social Problems Club. One of my contributions was to find and furnish a room where we could hold meetings, socialize, and read current magazines. I found friends in the Student Christian Movement because, surprisingly, that's where a lot of politics was discussed. Its president was a fervent communist, and I got involved in the struggle between his group and the opposing moderates. That was quite a lesson. The communists were well organized, doctrinaire, and considered themselves to be intellectuals. They talked intimidatingly about dialectical materialism and other subjects unknown to me. I was drawn toward the less militant group. I learned to develop my point of view and to hold my own in meetings and discussions.

I also had friends in the elite Letters Club, but it was closed to me, not only because it was limited to a small number of members (I think 20), but also because they discussed books that I didn't know existed, and which I wouldn't have had time to read. I wanted to write for the student newspaper, the *Ubyssey*, but that also turned out to be impossible. If you were going to be involved, you had to be a member of the staff and make a commitment to be there every day. For an engineering student with labs every afternoon, that was not possible. I must have made a nuisance of myself, because my efforts were recognized in the annual spoof issue with a letter to the editor signed Peter Limburger. There was also a fraternity scene, but quite apart from the fact that it required money, it held no interest for me, and I had no contact with it. Today the university has a reputation for being open and inclusive. When I was there, I felt hemmed in, partly because the social scene seemed not to be accessible to me, and because of the narrowness of the curriculum that I had chosen.

* * * * *

During the summers, I worked in the Transmission and Distribution Department of the British Columbia Electric Railway Company (BC Electric). My first job was as a "rail bond tester." I followed a courtly gentleman in suit and tie who carried an instrument to measure the electrical resistance between two rail segments, along with a little black book in which he marked the location of the bonds to be repaired. I held a bar in the shape of an upside-down T. At the junction of two rails each end of the T made contact with one of the rails so that the resistance between them could be measured.

Next, I was in substations, where the high-voltage transmission lines from the generating station connect to transformers whose output is at the lower voltage of the lines that go from pole to pole along the streets. I worked 48 hours a week, in shifts throughout the day and night that changed every week. Usually, I had sixteen hours between shifts, but sometimes there were only eight hours between leaving and coming back. Getting used to that, and to being at work from midnight to eight in the morning, was challenging. I worked at stations outside the city, along the Interurban lines of the BC Electric system. There was a journeyman electrician, a helper, and during the day also an engineer-in-charge (EiC), regulated by a union contract. Although I paid union dues, as a temporary helper I could not attend meetings. Again, I was part of a system and also excluded from it.

The first time the EiC showed me around, I pointed at something to ask what it was. He pushed my hand down and said, "We don't point around here." I learned that lesson well in my second substation, where the EiC's upper torso was one big scar. He had switched off two of the three breakers in one line to clean them, answered a phone call, and forgot to open the third one. He barely survived. After that, a rule required a signature to be deposited each time before one of the high-voltage units could be worked on.

Next summer, my job was to map wires along streets where they had hung so long that no one knew any longer where they went. I was shown the various numbers and sizes of the wires that I would encounter. I would be using a company car, but what my employers didn't know was that I didn't know how to drive. I found a driving school, and I was ready the following week. I was sent way out into the farmland. All went well until the car stopped and I couldn't get it restarted. I was stuck. After a while a farmer ambled over and tried to help. He spent a long time under the hood and finally came up to say, "You're out of gas." Gas? It hadn't occurred to me to think about that.

As I reflect on the long, supposedly educational process that I went through, I ask myself how much of that time was spent in worthwhile ways. There was so much that was pointless and inefficient, so much that was badly presented. I have to think that you are in luck if just a few courses or experiences turn out to be memorable and have lasting value. I questioned the process, and later, working toward a better system became a major part of my life.

GOOD BYE ENGINEERING, HELLO PHYSICS

After three years at UBC, I graduated as a Bachelor of Applied Science (BASc) in Electrical Engineering. At the graduation ceremony, the Canadian engineer's traditional iron ring was put on my finger by BC Electric's chief engineer. I had thought that, at that point, it would be imperative for me to get a job, but my parents were now established, and I was free to go my own way. My universe opened up, and I could choose which way to turn. That's when I changed my direction and turned to physics. I stayed at UBC for the next two years as a physics graduate student.

It seemed like a natural way to continue and to get a deeper look at what I knew already. The change turned out to be more drastic than that, and I stumbled into it without realizing the degree of the change in culture. It defined my further study and determined the shape of my life.

* * * * *

I am looking at my first physics book. Not much has survived from my days in Vienna. But here it is: *Du und die Natur—Eine Physik für Jedermann* (You and Nature, a Physics Book for Everyone), by Paul Karlson, 1934, inscribed with my name and the date, 1938. My parents must have given it to me when I was thirteen. I don't know whether it was in response to an expressed interest. I haven't looked at it in a long time, surprised that it took me only a few minutes to find it on my shelves.

The title equates physics with nature. You may find that strange, but it's just how I, and physicists in general, see nature. You understand a phenomenon at its deepest level when you know the forces between the parts of what you are dealing with and use the tools and thoughts of physics. Physics is most successful when it examines the structure of the simplest systems, such as the molecules, atoms, and nuclei of which matter is composed. That's when we can go the furthest and learn the most. Great progress has been made to take our knowledge to this deeper level. That's also where the subject becomes more detailed and more removed from common knowledge, leading to its reputation of being difficult.

I thumb through the book and remember some of its passages vividly. One that has stuck in my mind over the decades is about the Compton effect, which had been discovered in the previous decade. My memory is not of the dry technical description found in other books, showing that a light quantum can lose energy in a collision with an electron. It is, rather, the vivid remark that it is as if the light changed color when it collides, starting out blue, and becoming red after bouncing off. The usual description leads to a formula that describes this change. What impressed me went beyond the facts. It was that this was an unexpected and surprising result, which reinforced the then only recently developed quantum theory, and that the author was able to put it in simple and familiar terms.

As I look at the book now, I find it more readable than many of today's introductory books. The seed that it planted developed slowly and eventually came to fruition, not only as

I became a physicist, but in my dissatisfaction with the bloodless expositions which are the norm, and which I thought I could improve on as a teacher, and eventually by writing my own book.

Is that where my interest started? Or was it earlier, when I used a pair of scissors to cut a cord that was plugged in? Most of the current was short-circuited through the scissors, which had a notch taken out where the metal melted, leaving only a jolt for me. That may have been my first experience with experimental physics.

There is also a photo that couldn't have been taken much later, where I am playing at what the family called *kocherln,* an adaptation and diminutive of *kochen,* to cook. I am standing at a bench, seriously spooning sand and stones from one dish to another.

Later I had a kit with which to construct an electric motor. I wound a coil and mounted it between the poles of a horseshoe-shaped magnet. With a current through the coil from a battery, it turned, about half a turn. That was interesting, but not exactly exciting. The crucial part was to make the commutator. This is a switch which turns with the coil; it causes the direction of the current to reverse after half a turn, so that the coil turns through another half turn. And again, after another half, and so on. I understood what was supposed to happen, but to see the coil take off and start to turn rapidly was a thrilling experience.

* * * * *

I felt well prepared for the change to physics. Over the summer I studied a text on the structure of atoms and nuclei, which had not been part of my curriculum. I thought I knew enough about electricity, but I underestimated the gulf between the cultures of engineering and science. My usable knowledge was pretty much confined to what I had learned in my few physics courses, where I learned about the basic phenomena and the fundamental principles that allow us to understand them. Engineering stayed much closer to the surface, allowing calculations from tables and formulas without much examination of where they come from. It took me a long time to realize this and to get past my deficiencies.

I had missed the undergraduate courses of the physics curriculum, and that was a great disadvantage. At their best, they give a thorough examination of a subject, say electricity or optics, and provide the physical and mathematical tools that form the basis for further work or experimentation. It's a cliché that you learn a course when you teach it, but that was true for me. That's when you can take the subject matter apart and put it together in your own way so that it becomes your own. My aim was always to simplify, to look for the essence, the core meaning and contribution to knowledge, and to make it understandable. And not to let it get lost in the abstract, the mathematical overlay.

The graduate courses tended to be narrowly specialized and scattered in different directions. The main course that I remember from that time was in the electrical engineering department as one of two students. We read a book on electromagnetic waves with a young instructor to whom the subject matter seemed to be as new as it was to us.

The head of the physics department was Gordon Shrum, who was less a physicist than an organizer and entrepreneur. At UBC he was a major administrator. He hired faculty members from Europe and England, and laid the basis for a vibrant, modern department. Later he was dean of the graduate school, founded Simon Fraser University, and was instrumental in creating BC Hydro, the successor to BC Electric. While

I was there during wartime, he was also colonel and head of the Canadian Officers Training Corps (COTC), of which I was a less-than-warlike member.

I had a teaching assistantship, which paid my tuition, and a stipend of $600. I supervised sections of an elementary lab course like the one I never had. It was my first teaching job, and nobody told me what to do. I liked the interaction with the students, and it went well.

There were eight or ten of us new graduate students, ready to go on toward a master's degree in physics. (There was no PhD program at that time.) Shrum got us together to choose specialties and to apportion us to the faculty members who would supervise our research. I had only the remotest idea of what that was all about. I didn't know the professors, and I couldn't follow much of their brief accounts of their research. I was unaware that a good part of my life and activities were being decided.

By the time the session was over, I found myself in Kenneth C. Mann's group in nuclear physics. I was happy to be involved in a subject that interested me and was eager to learn more about it. The plan was to measure the emission of beta rays (electrons emitted by nuclei) and their spectra, i.e., the number emitted by a particular radioactive material at different energies. That's what I did for the following two years. Nuclear physics has remained more familiar to me than much that I encountered later.

For the first time I was free to take an elective. I chose economic geography with Harry Warren, which turned out to be more interesting and imaginative than what I was used to. I saw what a good teacher could do. Like his earlier course on mineralogy, this one had a lasting effect. He taught us how to look at the business section of a newspaper. As a geologist he wanted us to see past the financial manipulations that just push money from one place to another. He focused on natural resources, new materials, and new methods of using them. I still look for the real changes that are reported, rather than to the markets that depend on whims and perceptions.

Each student was asked to choose a publication to study and report on weekly. I chose *The Week in Review* of the *New York Times*. Years later, in a course at Rutgers that I called "The Science and Social Science of Energy," I used some of the same format and ideas.

* * * * *

How about life outside of classes during the years at UBC? The years of high school, working, and being in Winnipeg had made me more self-confident and outgoing by the time I got to UBC. The engineering students got together and sang songs that seemed to be mainly about drinking beer, but I had several close friends in the class who widened my range. These included Geoff, who had been in my high school class and was now studying mechanical engineering. He became a professor of aeronautical engineering at UBC, and I saw him whenever I was in Vancouver. The two friends I was closest to were fellow refugees, Julius from Poland, and Ervin from what is now the Czech Republic.

After graduation, I didn't see Julius again until our 50th reunion. Jaunty and cheerful as ever, he came with a young wife, now called himself Jake, and said he was an inventor. Ervin was the most Jewish-looking among us, which made it incongruous that his parents had converted to Christianity in an attempt to shield their children, and perhaps themselves, from the anti-Semitism they had experienced. Ervin and his sister took their conversion seriously. When I visited him some years later in Seattle, he told me about his family's

Bible study and church activities and asked about my interest in religion. It didn't take long to see that our views and activities had evolved so differently that we no longer had much in common. I did not see him again.

* * * * *

A postscript: In 1984, Lore and I stopped to spend a few days in Vienna on our way to a conference in Germany. This was the only time I returned to the city, and I thought I no longer knew anyone there. We were in a *pension*, the French word describing a small hotel with a breakfast room. The couple at the next table were talking about their visit to a craft museum that we also wanted to visit. I asked the man about it, and suddenly recognized him and said, "You took a picture of me years ago in Vancouver." It was the first husband of a Vancouver friend. He realized who I was, and that I knew much more about him, his former wife, her later husband, and their lives than he was likely to have told his companion, whom he was clearly trying to impress. It took only moments for him to get up, grab her, and flee.

* * * * *

During the summer after my first graduate year, the department was visited by the chair of the Yale physics department. He was upbeat, jovial, and got to know the three of us students who were working together. He assured us that we would have no problem getting accepted to Yale as graduate students. We were pleased with that, planned on it, and were stunned, when the time came, to get three rejection letters. Two of us had applied to other schools. One had nowhere else to go and asked to be put on Yale's waiting list. When fall came, he was accepted, and he was the first of our group to graduate.

The other two of us changed gears and went to our second-choice schools. I had no one to talk to about this and got my information from looking at graduate school catalogs. I applied to Columbia without thinking that I would actually go there. A member of the admissions staff passed through Vancouver and interviewed me. I described my work in nuclear physics with a confidence that seemed to impress him, and was accepted with a teaching assistantship that would pay for my tuition and living expenses. I was excited that I would be in New York and living at International House, just around the corner from the campus. The choice determined my subsequent professional and personal life. Whether it was the best choice remains debatable. Just how badly prepared I was would only become apparent later.

I had finished high school at sixteen and got credit for my first year of college through correspondence courses without much effort while I worked. After that my progress stalled, and it was about to stall more seriously now.

Some people move toward a goal in a straight line, but the path can be twisted and unpredictable. My first slowdown came from my choice of engineering, which seemed to make sense for me then, but wasted a lot of time and provided a poor start for what I did later.

The second slowdown was related to the first. I didn't understand how little I knew, and I went impatiently ahead. My friend at Yale told me that he was required to take a yearlong course in classical physics, which meant mechanics and other subjects that I considered boring and old-fashioned. I thought I already knew enough about them and was eager to get to more interesting material. I skipped the equivalent courses at Columbia, and there was no one to warn me that I was headed for trouble.

CHALK RIVER

After receiving our master's degrees, the three of us who had worked with the beta ray spectrometer were accepted as summer interns at the Canadian nuclear establishment in Chalk River, north of Ottawa. This was my first trip that far east since we arrived in Canada nine years earlier. Finally, I was going to be closer to what I thought of as the center of the world.

We were looking forward to working with a physicist who had a fine reputation as a scientist and as a person. We met with him, and he gave us our assignment, which was to make thin deposits of carbon on a substrate. He then left to follow his own summer plans, and we were on our own. Given our lack of experience and lack of communication with him, this was not a viable plan. We floundered around and basically got nothing done.

The centerpiece of the lab was the nuclear reactor. I was flabbergasted that I could walk around on top of its enclosure, knowing that only a few feet below me was the seething, deadly witches' brew of heavy water, neutrons, and uranium. Nothing of that could be seen, heard, or felt in the calm of the laboratory. By this time, I knew enough about nuclear physics to be able to follow a certain amount of what was going on.

Today I would be better at exploring and asking questions, but even then, I knew that I was close to the boundary between the known and the unknown.

* * * * *

There was little opportunity to explore our surroundings. We lived in dormitories in the isolated village of Deep River. I made some friends with other students. One invited me to spend a weekend with him and his family at their home in Montreal. I enjoyed the chance to get out, but was startled when he told me that it was the first time his family had become acquainted with someone who was Jewish.

One of the chemistry students was about to go to Princeton. I visited him there the following year, and he showed me around and told me how much he liked the university. I wonder what happened to him and to some of the others whose lives I wish I had followed.

One young woman from England already had a PhD and told me about the very different educational system that she had gone through. Her graduate study centered entirely on research toward the degree. No further courses were required. I thought that our education was broader and felt very superior about that.

One of the best-known physicists at Chalk River while I was there was Bruno Pontecorvo, who belonged to the group of Italian physicists who had worked with Enrico Fermi from 1934 to 1938, when they had done some of the first experiments with neutrons. Their work was groundbreaking, even though they missed the discovery of fission, despite looking right at it. I remember a short report by Pontecorvo with a description of inverse beta decay, a process that was later used in the first detection of neutrinos. He also had a string of other ideas to his credit. A short time later he disappeared, only to turn up in the Soviet Union. A recent biography suggests that his defection caused his extremely promising career effectively to come to an end.

It was a disappointment that my time at Chalk River was without a mentor or any other guidance. It was nevertheless a positive experience to get to know the laboratory with its people, the reactor, and the nature of the experiments that were done there. When I read or heard about a nuclear laboratory later, it was no longer an abstraction in a journal or a book. I had lived there. I understood something about its own special culture, even though I could look at it only from its periphery and again was not part of it.

* * * * *

At the end of the summer, I took the train to Montreal. The American Consulate in Vancouver had promised that my visa to the U.S. would be waiting for me there. When I got to the office and made my way to the head of the line, it became clear that they had never heard of me, and that I would have to start the application process all over. I all but camped there for three days. On receiving my visa, I was congratulated for having gone through the bureaucratic process so quickly.

I rushed to the train, got to New York, and finally met the professor who was to supervise my assistantship. By then, I was two days late and got a really ugly reception and lecture about my delinquency. That began my roller-coaster time at Columbia.

COLUMBIA

When I came to Columbia from Vancouver and Chalk River, I had a good deal of self-confidence and felt I could tackle anything. When I left about five years later, that confidence in myself and in the future was battered and severely tested. Once more, I was floating in unknown territory with no mentor, no one who would give me advice or guidance. I was getting a brand-name education. To be able to say that I was a Columbia student, and eventually that I had a Columbia degree, gave me an automatic stamp of approval. It did not describe what I actually knew. I eventually came away with an education, but I had largely to construct it myself over time.

In many departments the main hurdle is admission. Once you're there, the expectation is that you will graduate, and that the faculty has some responsibility to help you. That was not so here. Columbia admitted more than would graduate and weeded them out through its PhD qualifying examination. My grades after the first semester were not good, and when I told Polykarp Kusch, the professor in charge of the exam, that I wanted to take it at the end of the second semester, his doubt was obvious. I took it and passed, and he even commended me when he saw me later.

I. I. Rabi was head of the department. There was no pretense of democracy by calling him the "chair." He was in charge. And not an easygoing person. Another Canadian student and I talked to him at the single departmental party of those years, where his comment to us was, "Columbia gets lots of foreign students, and they all come with glowing recommendations, but when they get here, we see that they don't know anything." When one of my friends went to him to apply for a fellowship, he told him, "I can't think of any reason why you should get this fellowship."

After I graduated, I had the opportunity to talk with him in a more relaxed way at a dinner following a talk he gave. He came across as more human, but very conservative in his attitudes.

In my first semester I took Rabi's course in atomic physics. He did not have a good reputation as a teacher, made mistakes in mathematical developments, and was not well organized. But I liked the class because it went beyond the grubby details to the physical essence. I took good notes and thought I learned a lot. A few weeks before the end of the course, he left to take up his other role as elder statesman and advisor to the federal government. The instructor who took over from him gave a completely different and much less captivating course, and I never made the necessary adjustment. Following this and my other courses, that semester was made especially trying by the absence of any textbook that might have provided support.

I knew I wanted and needed a course in quantum mechanics because this is the basis for all modern knowledge of the structure of matter. In Vancouver I got only a poor introduction to it. Here the course was given by Willis Lamb, again a world-renowned physicist on his path to a Nobel Prize. It may well have been a good course for the right student, but not for me. Not only that, but Lamb decided to spend the last part of the course on the application of group theory to quantum mechanics. I was working as hard as I could and decided not to study that part of the subject at all, in order to concentrate on the rest. It was not a good strategy. The exam was primarily on the material that I had put aside.

The third course was classical mechanics, mostly from the 19th century. It met for two hours once a week. When the bell rang, the door opened and Professor Quimby came in, talking. He went to the blackboard, picked up a piece of chalk and continued to talk while he filled the several blackboard segments, starting from the top-left corner. When he came to the bottom-right corner, he erased it all and started again from the top. He continued to talk and write until the bell rang two hours later, when he put down the chalk and left. Again, no textbook, no support. I got a good grade, but not a good grasp of the subject.

Many graduate students in the Columbia Physics Department around that time felt that life there was difficult and sometimes traumatizing. On the other hand, there were also those to whom the fast pace and the presence of a star faculty gave a great start to their careers. I hated the constant pressure of exams and grades. Columbia even had a second open-ended exam, where the questions were again limited only by the imagination of the faculty. I sometimes got bad grades when I thought I knew the material. I also occasionally got good grades in subjects where I thought my knowledge was superficial. My persistence helped, but my knowledge was fragmented.

Some students knew how to do all the homework problems and those on the tests. They were the professors' darlings. And sometimes it turned out that this was all they could do. I am thinking of a few I knew later, when they had become faculty members themselves. They knew the standard material. But they lacked initiative, imagination, and insight, and their work and careers got stuck and never came to fruition.

My salary as a teaching assistant ($1200 and free tuition) allowed me to live at International House, around the corner from the campus, and pay for incidentals. Money was tight, and it was quite a day when I was offered a research assistantship after I passed the qualifying exam. It was with the group that I had started to work with, nominally headed by John Dunning, who had done some of the earliest work on fission. The pay was going to be twice as much as my teaching assistantship. I reported this to my TA supervisor, again Kusch, who said, "You're one of my few senior assistants, and I can't let you go."

I had no choice. It was a compliment, after all, from Kusch, a gruff but not unkind man, soon another winner of the Nobel Prize. The raise had to wait for another year.

I supplemented my earnings by tutoring. For some time, one student provided a steady income for me and for a chemistry graduate student. His family was willing to pay for our services, including the time for the subway ride to farthest Brooklyn where they lived. With our help, he was able to graduate, something it is unlikely he could have done on his own. He encouraged us to raid the refrigerator, and we did not hesitate, even while we knew we were not doing society any favors by preparing him for work for which he was not suited.

Another source of income was the translation of scientific articles from German to English through agencies in tiny downtown offices run by refugees who brought nothing with them except their knowledge of languages. I started with one that paid a quarter of a cent per word and ended with another that paid four times as much. At the beginning, I wrote the translation out a couple of times. Later, I tried to save time by typing the final copy as I translated directly from the original. Doing this late at night did not always allow me to adjust my syntax, and I remember being told by one of my employers when he looked at my work, "This is not English, this is German!"

The money I earned was not sufficient for regular dental care, especially when it turned out that several earlier fillings needed to be replaced. I was saved by the New York University Dental Clinic, where I had to sign up to be available on their schedule. The work was done by students under close supervision by an army of instructors, and it led to some hair-raising experiences. I can still feel the first injection that my sweating student ever gave, as the instructor said, "No, no, not there!" — and his first experience with a root canal. Years later a "real" dentist looked at my teeth and said, "I guess I'd give him a C." Nevertheless, his work took care of me for a long time.

* * * * *

The research enterprise was another part of my life that contributed to my feeling of being on a roller coaster. I had some experience with beta ray spectroscopy at UBC, and it seemed both natural and efficient to continue with it, especially since two groups at Columbia were working on this subject. One group was that of C. S. Wu. Every experiment that she did with her students was interesting and inventive, shedding light on aspects that had previously not been understood. When I was there, she was a research associate, not even a faculty member, but eventually she earned the highest accolades for her successes. She didn't get the Nobel Prize, although many people, and by all accounts she herself, thought she should have.

Perhaps that's worth a digression. C. S. Wu is most famous

for the experiment that showed that beta rays are not emitted by nuclei equally in all directions. It had been assumed that there was no preferred direction until T. D. Lee and C. N. Yang pointed out that there seemed to be no law preventing the electrons from being emitted asymmetrically.

It's a long way from a theoretical suggestion to a complex experiment that shows what is actually happening. Further discouraging in this case was the likelihood that nothing unusual would be observed. The nuclei must be lined up in one direction, which can be done at very low temperatures in a magnetic field. The distribution of the emitted electrons can then be measured under these difficult circumstances. Wu did the measurement and showed that there is indeed a large difference in the emission in different directions.

The experiment led to new and fundamental insights. It depended on Wu's skills, and also on those of a group at what was then called the National Bureau of Standards, who were pioneers in the techniques of aligning nuclei. How much credit did they deserve? And other experiments were closing in on the same result. In any case, Lee and Yang got the Prize and she did not. Was that an example of priority given to theoretical conjecture over meticulous and difficult experimentation? Or did the result depend on too many other people who might have deserved a share? To what extent did she not get the respect that she deserved because she was a woman?

I see that I keep mentioning Nobel Prizes. There are other prizes and some even come with as much money. But the Nobel Prize is in a category by itself, representing the highest recognition. There are differences: sometimes one is given for an expected result, but the best open a new field or present a previously unknown insight. The award can be controversial and, as with other honors and prizes, there is a political component. But it represents unique achievement. It's a rare department that has even one, and hardly any that have as many as I came across at Columbia.

* * * * *

The second group investigating beta rays in the department consisted of two graduate students with a nominal supervisor who, however, did not seem to pay any attention to them. The project they were engaged in seemed close to what I knew and understood, and I fell in with them without exploring other opportunities. It was another questionable decision.

The relationship between a PhD mentor and student is often close and the German term *Doctorvater* (Doctorfather) emphasizes its influence which often goes beyond the time as a student, and can determine his or her direction and subsequent progress.

In my first research venture at Columbia there were only the two students. One was about to finish his PhD work on the beta ray spectrum of a radioactive material with a half-life of less than a second. That meant producing the material in the Columbia cyclotron and making the measurements right away, before it comes apart. He graduated, became a scientist in a National Laboratory, and later achieved prominence in public life.

I was left with the other student, Victor. The arrangement was that I would help him with his thesis, and then he would help me with mine. The first part worked, but then the well seemed to run dry. We consulted a visiting physicist, who was appalled that we got so little help, and made some suggestions that also led nowhere.

At that point a new star streaked across the Columbia sky: Jack Steinberger, just a few years older than I, a refugee from Germany, and clearly an extraordinary physicist. I asked him whether I could work with him, and he said no. He had already taken on several students ("stolen them," as he said), and would surely be fired if there were more. Later he relented and became my thesis supervisor, which would be on the lifetime measurement of particles produced by what was then the largest cyclotron in the world.

As a blessing, this was mixed. He didn't really do any supervising. Jack thought and worked faster than anyone, and he drove relentlessly toward results. He wasn't going to stop to look over his shoulder to see whether I was there and knew what was going on. After a couple of years, he said, "OK, this can be your thesis," and I spent the next months reading about it and studying the background. I even made a small calculation that helped, and I wrote it up.

Jack tolerated me, but there were some rough times. Once he asked me to bring a piece of equipment from the physics building to Columbia's Nevis Cyclotron Lab north of New York. I was to hold it on the truck while we made our slow way north. He was very proud of having designed the device, and went to the machine shop every day while it was being built. It was an insulated container, like a thermos bottle, with a thin window through which liquid hydrogen could be bombarded with particles from the cyclotron. I got there early on the appointed morning, ready to hang onto it in the pouring rain. The machinists who had built it and put it on the truck laughed and said they had tied it down and covered it so that it couldn't budge, and for me just to ride in the cab with the driver.

When we got to the lab, Jack ran out gleefully to pat his baby, saying to me in passing, "Sorry you got wet." Quite unnecessarily I said I had been in the cab. He turned on me furiously and berated me for not staying with the precious cargo.

We still had to make the liquid hydrogen, a process that

usually requires specialized training. This was done in a shed outside the physics building because it is too dangerous to use the flammable hydrogen inside. The group assembled there one morning, with Jack holding a sheaf of papers describing the sequence that we were to follow. The faculty member usually in charge of this quite complicated operation had left the instructions and seemed to have left town. Neither Jack nor any of the rest of us had any experience with low temperatures like that of liquid hydrogen, 20 degrees above absolute zero. The hydrogen was initially a gas in high-pressure tanks on a mezzanine platform accessible only via a rickety ladder. When the liquefaction procedure came to the point where the hydrogen gas was to be let out of the tanks, Jack looked around and I found myself climbing up the ladder to open the valve to the tanks when he gave the signal at the appointed moment.

Everything worked, as Jack read out the instructions to open and close valves, measure temperatures, and check containers, and finally the liquid hydrogen was bubbling in its container. There was just one more jaw-clenching moment. At the top of an open vessel that is cold enough, air can condense, become solid, fall in, and clog the narrow opening.

When that happens, with hydrogen boiling away in its container and no way for the gas to escape the clogged vessel, you are on your way to a hydrogen explosion. Jack, more alert and aware than anyone else, noticed that this was happening, grabbed a brass bar, and pushed it down into the hydrogen container to open it up and let the gas escape.

I tried as hard as I could to follow and understand Jack's work and his plans. One day he was in the lab, working on the kind of metal structure that was the main component of electronic equipment at the time. It held vacuum tubes and other components that had to be individually connected. It was before the time of transistors or circuit boards. You would turn the whole thing upside down on a bench to solder wires and to measure voltages. I went to look over his shoulder to glean some wisdom from the master. This lasted about two seconds. He turned and said, "No, we're not going to do this," and told me how he had started at the University of Chicago with someone who would say, "Now we're going to attach this wire," or "Now we're going to turn this knob," and so on. He said he'd fled as soon as he could, and he wasn't about to do that sort of thing now.

There was also the time when he took a carful of us to Brookhaven National Laboratory for a tour. When we got there, he realized that I was not a U.S. citizen, and I spent the whole day in his apartment.

Jack and his methods were satirized at one of the rare social events of the lab. The student (whom I will call Bill) who played the role of Jack went around and simulated taking equipment from other people's work stations. Jack watched glumly, hunched over with his head almost between his knees. Somebody went over to him and said, "You're not laughing. This is supposed to be fun." His answer was, "I don't have to laugh, I'm the butt!"

The same student was rather brash and known for talking back and being independent. Not everyone admired that. There was one faculty member who was sort of an assistant to Jack. I had hoped he would be a buffer between us, someone I could go to for information and explanations, but that didn't happen. One time he looked at Bill and said, "That guy should never be in a laboratory." Bill, on the other hand, said to me, "Look at them, they're no smarter than I am, and every one of them is a full professor." And sure enough, he became an active and well-known professor at a good university.

My mother came to visit, and I proudly showed her around.

She looked at the tangle of wires and electronic equipment on the messy benches and the floor, and said with dismay, "This is your laboratory?" I guess she expected the super-clean rooms and white-coated personnel of her own experience.

While I worked on the last part of my thesis, I looked for a temporary job. One place where I applied was what was then called the New York State Merchant Marine Academy. It was where the Throgs Neck Bridge is now, and it took a while to get there. You had to take a subway to the end of the line, then a bus to the end of its route, and walk a mile farther to where a ship was tied up. I spent some hours with the head of the physics department as he showed me around, while students came up, saluting before they talked, everyone in uniform. I thought I could get used to that as I considered the good features: a better than usual salary and the possibility of signing on as assistant purser during the summer while the ship went around the world. I was disappointed when I got a rejection letter. When I told Jack, he said, "What, you didn't even get that job?" It didn't make this my best day.

None of these experiences kept him from writing a letter of recommendation when I graduated that was instrumental in getting me the job at Rutgers that I had for the next 46 years.

I saw him again years later at a reception when he got the Nobel Prize. We shook hands and he leaned forward conspiratorially to say, "Remind me what we did together." He obviously had no memory of it or, thankfully, of anything else about me. I told him that it was on the fraction of times that neutral pions decayed into a gamma ray and an electron pair, rather than into the more usual two gamma rays. "Ah," he said, "not the worst experiment that I've been involved with."

Years later still, I sent him a copy of my physics book and suggested that he might say something about it that I could use for publicity. He demurred, saying that he knew nothing about physics education, but in the end gave it a delightful endorsement.

* * * * *

The temporary job that I did get was at Drew University in Madison, New Jersey. Marshall Harrington, their one physics professor, had been there for decades. It's not clear whether he had ever left New Jersey. He was born there, spent his vacations at the New Jersey shore, and had his degree from Princeton. For this year, however, he had been offered a position under UNESCO sponsorship as head of the physics department in Baghdad, and I was his replacement. He stayed a second year, with another graduate student replacing him, and when he came back to the U.S., it was not to Drew. I guess he had seen the world and wanted more of it.

I liked Drew. It was a friendly place, and I had more responsibility there than I would have again for a long time. I taught the single physics course, and I was all there was in the department, except for Mr. Donaldson, who kept the equipment clean and took it out for the student experiments.

* * * * *

While I was at Drew I started thinking about longer-lasting positions. One day at Columbia, I crossed paths in the hallway with the department head at the time, Charles Townes, the person primarily responsible for the invention of the laser and its forerunner, the maser. I wasn't sure he knew who I was, but he stopped me and said, "How would you like a job at Rutgers?" I said yes, even though I didn't even know what or where it was. I soon found out, asked people about it, and was told about the good work done there by Bernard Serin in superconductivity. I applied, got invited, gave a talk about my work, and got the job as instructor.

* * * * *

The moment that marks the end of the road toward the PhD at Columbia is the conclusion of the formal final oral exam in the Trustees Room in Low Library. Jack looked for the chair with the plaque showing that it was for Thomas J. Watson, the head of IBM, whose name is also that of an important Columbia laboratory, and the rest of the committee found their places on other pieces of the heavy furniture.

I must have started with an exposition of the thesis, but I have no memory of that. T. D. Lee asked a question, and as soon as he did, I relaxed because I saw that I knew what to say. It was only after the exam that he told me that he was thinking of a more subtle aspect than the one to which I responded. James Rainwater, another member of the physics faculty, had a criticism of something I had calculated, but mercifully suggested that I could fix that and submit it to him later without waiting for another exam date. The well-known chemist Victor K. LaMer asked me to explain what a standard deviation is. I knew that, but as I gave my answer, I realized that it came close to exhausting my knowledge of statistics, and that the next member of the committee was a statistician. When his turn came, he looked up briefly from the stack of papers he had been grading and said, "Since the statistical question has already been answered, I have nothing further." I was done.

As I think back, I have to ask myself whether Columbia was the best place for me. I made mistakes in my choice of courses, and later in my choice of research projects.

I turned down the opportunity to continue in the field of

my thesis because the machines were getting larger and the groups more impersonal. And my memories and experiences with work in that field were not so great. After I graduated, I felt I could do whatever I wanted. This optimism did not take into account that the transition to a new field would turn out to take longer than I had expected.

I could see that my fellow graduate students had a head start if they continued in the field of their thesis. Today all hiring in research departments, such as that at Rutgers, is based on work the applicant has already done in a particular field as a student or postdoc. The expectation is that the new recruit will advance the work and reputation of the department in that field. That was not so for my new colleague Duke Sells and me. Neither of us had experience in a field that the department wanted to pursue at that time. We were hired as "instructors," a rank so low that it is no longer used. We eventually learned, at our peril, that the department did not look at us as lasting additions.

INTERNATIONAL HOUSE AND BEYOND

I liked being in New York. I lived at International House for two years, and that was as good a base as I can imagine. I had a room to myself, and I didn't have to live in a student dormitory. I had a social life with friends and activities. Even with the pressures of classes and research, I got around quite a bit. Going to the Museum of Modern Art didn't cost as much as it does now, and I-House had discount tickets to Broadway shows. My salary as a teaching assistant took care of my living expenses and these frills, plus trips to New Haven and Princeton to visit friends from earlier times. I also spent time on yet another roller coaster, the quest for female companionship.

My best friend George Schillinger was more worldly than I, and that helped me to meet people. He became the I-House student president. On one memorable occasion he was invited to spend a weekend at the home of Farnsworth W. Loomis in Greenwich, Connecticut, and told he could bring a friend.

"Farnie" was a biologist who worked in his own laboratory. He was a member of a family known for funding their own research and making many contributions to science. He and his family were extraordinarily warm and hospitable to us. At the end of the weekend, he told George that he wanted to finance his education as far as he wanted to go. George asked what he could do in return, and Farnie answered that the day might come when he would be able to help a younger person in a similar way. I was impressed, and later followed that suggestion myself.

After our two years at I-House, George and I found an apartment close by that we shared for the next two years. Life became more stressful for me when George's girlfriend Mary moved in. Actually, there was no problem, except that I was more aware of my aloneness. I was best man at their wedding, but the marriage did not last.

Among the people with whom I had contact at I-House was Aage Bohr, the son of one of the most revered physicists of the century, Niels Bohr, the first to have described atoms as consisting of nuclei and electrons. Aage had the room next to mine, and I asked him what was of particular interest to him at Columbia. "Ah, what Rainwater is doing is very interesting." James Rainwater had recently written a very short letter to the *Physical Review*, with the description of a possible new aspect of the structure of nuclei. When he returned to Denmark, Aage worked on this question with a colleague. When I turned on the radio one morning a few years later and heard that an American and two Danes had won the Nobel Prize, I had no doubt who they were.

Leontyne Price was from Mississippi, a student at Julliard, at the very beginning of her career as an opera singer. I got to know her through my friend, Barbara.

Barbara and I were comfortable with each other, even though we came from such different backgrounds—she African-American, and I a Jewish refugee from Vienna. I liked walking with her along 125th Street (sometimes called Harlem's Main Street), or for that matter, down Fifth Avenue. We talked about our upbringings, our families, and everything else. The Black-and-White thing was a presence but not an issue. When I got an invitation to visit a couple who were friends of my parents, I took her along. A little later my mother came for a visit, and Barbara was with us when we went out together.

I was stunned by their reactions. The husband of the couple we visited wrote a letter severely admonishing me for bringing Barbara. But it was my liberal mother to whom I had always looked up, and who had been such a role model for me, who was the biggest disappointment. She really had no criticism of Barbara other than a rude remark about her weight. Barbara was good-looking, but no waif. My father got wind of the story and wrote, "You can't do this to me." I was outraged by these comments. They were difficult for Barbara and me, but they also brought us closer. We talked about them, and we continued to see each other. Sometime later, I realized that I was losing my confidence. My mother's opposition played a role and so did my continuing difficulty to make any commitments.

There was also the girl who, on our first date, announced that she had already picked out the pattern for her silverware. I ran away as fast as I could. Another first date collapsed at a Broadway play. I was happy to be there with the young woman, but she must have thought that I was too excited and talkative. At any rate, on the way back she said coldly, "I don't want to sleep with you." We were many miles away from anything of the sort. But it was a conversation stopper.

* * * * *

The next encounter was different. It was my second year at I-House. I was in my room studying to prepare for more exams when Bill Hardy, a fellow physics graduate student, came by with, "You've got to get out of here." I replied, "No, leave me alone. I have to study," although I wanted nothing more than to get away. "Come with me! I'm going to a club!" I had no idea what he was talking about, but I wasn't hard to persuade. He took me to the *Eighth Street Club*, which became a legendary institution, on an evening that itself became legendary. He introduced me to people, some of whose names I recognized as artists, musicians, sculptors, and dancers—Bill de Kooning, John Cage, Merce Cunningham, and others far from famous at the time, but who changed the course of 20th century art.

The evening's program consisted of a talk by John Cage that entered history as a "Non-Lecture." There were few chairs, and most of the audience stood. He spoke, but stopped from time to time. The audience was left to wonder whether there was more. It was stop-and-go, just like some of his music. It wasn't easy to follow the trend of his thought, or even to determine whether there was one.

Bill also introduced me to Lore Kadden, who had come to know this group at *Black Mountain College*, the small avant-garde, art-oriented college from which she graduated. We went out a few times, but then we didn't see each other for about two years. After that time of studying and ineffective floating, I sent her a Valentine's Day card that I had made. I don't remember anything about it, but I did get a response, a scallop shell that she had decorated, which I still have.

* * * * *

There were many similarities between Lore's background and mine. She was brought up in northern Germany, in the industrial town of *Wuppertal*. Her father was a small businessman (I never found out just what he did), and her mother had been his bookkeeper. When I met Lore, I did not realize that she came from a Jewish family, and it was not one of my concerns. In the First World War, her father had held a top non-commissioned rank in the German army (*Vizefeldwebel*) which, for a Jew, was very unusual. There were many Jewish officers, but rarely NCOs. He prided himself on his military experience, and when Hitler came to power he pinned on his medals. Like so many, he thought that this would demonstrate his allegiance to the state and shield him from persecution.

Both he and Lore's mother came from observant Jewish homes and continued many of the traditions. At the same time the family considered themselves to be German, as illustrated by their given names (Alfred and Frieda) and those that they gave to their children (Kurt and Hannelore). Like my father he was convinced that the madness couldn't last, and the family stayed until *Kristallnacht* ("the night of broken glass," November 9, 1938) showed the futility of that assumption. Lore, then seventeen years old, was at school when she was warned not to go home. One of her mother's brothers had earlier moved to Holland, across the nearby border, and that's where the family fled to. There, Lore began working in a high-class dress shop where clothes were made for the queen, and later attributed her strong sewing skills to the training she received there.

Relatives helped them get to the United States so that they avoided getting trapped in the countries that were soon occupied by Nazi Germany. They settled in the Boston area and Lore's father became a salesman. He went to offices and small factories to sell housewares to the women employees for small weekly or monthly payments, no doubt at high rates of interest. Lore's brother enlisted in the army and became a citizen right away. After the war he joined his father as a salesman. Lore went to work at the *Window Shop* which had been started by a group of Harvard faculty wives as a place where refugee women could serve coffee and pastries and sell craft objects and clothes that they made. She was a salesgirl. She also suggested work that would be acceptable in the American market. She had gone to art school in Germany, and already had the extraordinary sense of style and design that characterized everything that she did later.

She took evening courses in English, and at one time saw a poster describing the program of the Wellesley Institute for Social Progress. While she was looking at it, a woman came up, started talking with her, and mentioned that she might want to apply for a scholarship to attend the Institute. Lore did that, and the woman, who turned out to be the director of the Institute, Dorothy Hill, became a mentor and major influence.

When the Window Shop began to give retirement benefits to its employees, Dorothy suggested that Lore ask instead for help to go to college. She was in her twenties, and very ready to get away from the narrow life with her parents. The home atmosphere was stifling, without any encouragement for her to develop her talents or further her education.

She learned about Black Mountain College, the avant-garde college in North Carolina that emphasized art, which turned out to be ideal for her. The three years she spent there shaped her life. She soaked up the adventurous spirit, the experimental program, and found the teaching and leadership, to a large extent by recent refugees from central Europe, exciting and congenial.

The Window Shop paid for the first year, but then told her that they did not have the resources to renew the scholarship. Lore was preparing to leave, when she met Mrs. Anna Jamieson, the mother of a former student, who was visiting the college. After Mrs. Jamieson returned home, she wrote to

Lore that she wanted to fund her studies at the college for as long as she wished to attend.

I later met her, as well as Dorothy Hill, older women who gave me a glimpse of a segment of society I had not known. They were engaged with the world and prepared to help others where they could. They were the opposite of glamorous, wearing black dresses and plain hats. But they radiated an extraordinary strength of character. I think of them as part of the bedrock of America.

Josef Albers, known primarily as a painter, was the leading spirit at Black Mountain College when Lore was there. He developed a course in design that became the model for others across the country, and his wife, Anni, was perhaps the preeminent American weaver of her generation. Both had been at the Bauhaus in Germany, the most innovative and famous art school in Europe until it was forced to close when Hitler came to power, and they brought its avant-garde heritage to America.

Lore took Josef Albers' course three times, and her meticulous notes are now in the collection of the Albers Foundation. She specialized in weaving, with Anni as her mentor, and graduated following an exhibition of her work. One of Lore's pieces from that time and a weaving of Anni's were the leading pieces in an exhibit called "High Fiber" in 2005 at the Renwick Gallery in Washington, DC, which is part of the Smithsonian American Art Museum.

BMC was an incubator for some of the most modern and avant-garde art in the U.S. in the 20th century. For summer sessions, Albers invited artists who later became well known, such as choreographer Merce Cunningham and his partner, the composer John Cage. Buckminster Fuller came with the design for his first geodesic dome. He tried to put it up with a group of students, including Lore, but it collapsed. He redesigned it, and it was reconstructed the next year, this time as a stable structure. The painter Robert Rauschenberg was a fellow student. The sculptor Ruth Asawa was a close friend. Much later we visited Ruth and her family in San Francisco, and she took us on a memorable tour of the half dozen or so fountains in the city that are her work. The iconoclastic painter Willem de Kooning was at the college, as well as the photographer Aaron Suskind, who gave Lore a photograph. I was surprised that this was the only piece of art of any value that she came away with. When I asked her about that, she stood still for a moment and looked into the distance. "I guess I wasn't willing to pay the price," was her comment.

Legions of relationships flourished at BMC, but Lore seems to have waved off every man who might have come close to her, including de Kooning and Suskind. "I knew I would be thrown away after a few weeks," she said. Not many others came out of the college without having had a romantic attachment. If she had, she might not have been ready for me when I met her. On the other hand, it showed her difficulty with lowering her guard. I think she was fearful of losing control. Albers must have seen this when he said, "What you need is *Schnapps!*"

Heinrich Jalowetz headed the music department. He had worked with Arnold Schoenberg, the Austrian composer who, perhaps more than anyone, exemplified the break with the classical tradition. He collapsed and died while he was conducting a concert at the college early in Lore's stay. She was close to his widow Johanna and their two daughters. The older one, Trude, a renowned weaver, took Anni's place at the college while the Albers were in Mexico for a year. Her sister Lisa married the Broadway set designer Boris Aronson and worked with him. I shared these friendships, especially with Lisa, whose son and his wife and their two sons have remained close friends. Altogether, the BMC influence was foundational for Lore and shaped her outlook on art and design, as well as her professional life, and to some extent her personal life. After our marriage, I participated vicariously in much of this experience.

When Lore was about to leave BMC for New York, some of the faculty and students said, "When you are there, you must come to our club." That turned out to be the 8th Street Club where, as a result of the most unlikely series of events, I met her.

* * * * *

Lore and I began to see each other, and she eventually invited me to dinner in her one-room apartment on 89th Street, together with her friend Lisa Aronson. Lisa's presence as what she later called a chaperone made the atmosphere more relaxed than it might have been. This was the year that I was at Drew, and after some time I began to drive to New York in my first car, a 1936 Chevy, to spend the weekends with Lore. She worked as a textile designer, using the loom that took up most of the space in her apartment. She said she had all week to think of the menu for our evenings together.

She would also have a bottle of wine, of which she drank a good deal less than I did. The wine helped to break down my shell and my defenses, and after some time I asked her whether she would like to get married to me. She answered, "That would make me very happy." Given the place, the time, and the wine, I wasn't sure that she thought I was serious, but when I came the next time with flowers and champagne, the question was settled. We talked about when, and she was startled when I suggested the end of the spring semester when I would be finished at Drew. She was ready right then and there. But I needed some time to get used to the idea that my life was going to be completely overturned.

We went to see Rabbi Hoffman, a chaplain at Columbia, and found him congenial. We talked about the ceremony, and he was very flexible. We asked him to leave out some of the traditional features, such as the crushing of the glass when you swear that you will never forget Jerusalem. Lore asked for a *chupah*, the wedding canopy that she thought of as the enveloping shawl in Chagall paintings. The rabbi said yes, they had one. It turned out to be four high poles topped with what Lore thought looked more like a handkerchief. Four of our friends held the poles at the ceremony, and we were very happy.

Lisa and her husband Boris offered their apartment for a reception of about 40 guests. It was on Columbus Circle in a building later replaced by the Coliseum which, in turn, was eventually torn down. My mother came from Vancouver, and Lore's parents from Boston. It was quite wonderful for us.

The real world at last: Lore with Tommy and Naomi

PART 4: THE REAL WORLD AT LAST

ADULTHOOD

Finally, I became an adult. It was 1953, I came to the end of my formal education, we got married and moved to our own apartment. I had a job and more control over my life. The change to independence and responsibility was huge.

My marriage to Lore was the source of great joys, and it also gave rise to serious difficulties. In my work I had times of great satisfaction; others of missteps and setbacks. As I look back, I ask myself how the good parts could have been made better and the bad parts avoided. Perhaps there is some value in reflection, illumination, and understanding.

I was excited about coming to Rutgers. I thought I knew the terms of my employment but soon found out that there were aspects that I did not anticipate. To start with, I was assigned to supervise laboratories and problem sessions just like those that I had dealt with as a teaching assistant at UBC and Columbia. That was no great challenge, and I was eager for more interesting work.

I soon realized that I and Robert "Duke" Sells, the other instructor who came to the department at the same time as I, were scheduled to teach twice as many hours as any of the rest of the faculty. Their "load" was reduced as part of the grant to further the department's research. I was further rattled when, about a month after I started, I received a letter to remind me that my appointment was for one year, and there was no guarantee that the appointment would be renewed. My colleagues tried to reassure me, but that did not change the letter and its harsh tone.

I was hired for a specific task. Radioactive materials were still fairly new in university and industrial laboratories, and a member of the department, Frank Dunnington, had started a project to encourage their use. He had raised funds from local companies, such as Johnson & Johnson, the drug and medical company, and the oil company that was later called Exxon. Seymour Zenchelsky, a member of the chemistry faculty, and I were to design and set up a laboratory and teach a course which would be a prerequisite for every user of radioactive materials in the university. We made the preparations, bought the equipment, and started the course. I gave the lectures on nuclear structure and radioactivity. The lab covered measurements of radioactivity and techniques of handling radioactive materials.

I was happy to have a responsible and independent activity. It also meant that in my first serious course most students were much older than I. I tried to find the right tone, somewhere between polite deference and authority. We didn't give grades. It helped that I knew the subject really well.

Between the sections of the elementary laboratories and the new course, my time was completely taken up, but I wanted to get started on a research project, even though I was only dimly aware of how essential this was if I was to stay at Rutgers.

Before the war, the physics department consisted of four members. When I arrived in 1953, three of them were still there, including Frank, who had been asked in the late 1940s to create a modern department, with faculty engaged in research at the forefront of physics. When I came, the department had already taken steps toward greater research capabilities and received a government grant that freed faculty from some of their teaching duties and paid for some major research equipment.

This was the heyday of public and government support for physics. Physicists, including new graduates, found positions in government and industrial laboratories and in colleges and universities. Government labs such as Brookhaven and Oak Ridge were known for their contributions to the development of nuclear bombs, radar, and other technical work related to the war. Industrial labs, such as RCA, Bell Labs, and General Electric, were hotbeds of invention that led to television and the rest of the electronics revolution. Universities participated in this tide, fueled by government grants, partly to the institutions and partly to individual faculty members.

Frank hired people mostly from other universities. When I came, about half a dozen of them, already with substantial accomplishments to their credit, were now the dominant group in the department, an oligarchy that ruled by consensus among themselves. Their main occupation, and the subject of their ambition, was their research. Teaching was taken seriously, but the message was clear: favors, bonuses, and promotions were given almost exclusively for research accomplishments.

One of my fellow graduate students had started as a postdoctoral fellow at a well-known university and was now in a faculty position. His earlier job was open, and he suggested that I follow in his footsteps; this would allow me to continue in the field of my thesis as most graduates wanted to do. It meant working with ever-larger machines, in ever-larger groups in which individual work was submerged. I didn't apply.

Nor did I try for the industrial labs where jobs were plentiful and had major advantages. The salaries were higher than at universities, and you didn't have to scramble for research funds when you got there. The best prided themselves on the freedom that they gave to their staff to pursue projects whose payoffs, if any, would materialize only later. But spending time in a cubicle, with equipment but limited contact with people, was not what I was looking for.

The situation is different today. Starting positions at research universities go to those who already have experience and accomplishments in a field where the institution wants to start or expand. Most often they have already had postdoc positions. The road I took no longer exists.

Frank had been chairman of the department that he had built, but the others found him to be dictatorial, uncommunicative, and difficult to work with. They revolted and asked the administration to remove him as chair. By the time I arrived, Charlie Whitmer, the mildest member of the group, had replaced him. The department became harmonious, but at a cost: every decision, including where a chair or a mailbox should be placed, was now discussed in a faculty meeting.

Although I didn't know it at the time, the ruling group didn't hesitate to fire junior colleagues who did not live up to the new research-oriented image. That aspect was hidden by the generally collegial and supportive atmosphere. Charlie and his wife, Jeanette, held an open house once a month. She was a very organized person, who made Charlie's lunches to be stored in the freezer for a month at a time. The evenings followed an unchanging pattern. There were party games, for which you had to have a certain aptitude. Graduate students liked them, and faculty wives did not. In one such game you moved from chair to chair, but the chairs retained the names of the people who sat on them initially, which you had to remember. Lore quickly ran into trouble when she blurted out her maiden name, which no one knew since she had abandoned it when we married just a few months earlier. The games were followed by coffee and pie. Jeanette found out that Lore had never baked a pie and arranged a lesson. Lore came home with hers, and it remained the only one she ever made.

It soon became clear that a more forceful person was required, someone who would steer the department toward research at the highest level. Henry Torrey had the most prominent research reputation, and he became chair. He had been the co-discoverer at Harvard of nuclear magnetic resonance, the forerunner of what is now called, in deference to the popular fear of the word nuclear, magnetic resonance imaging. He came within shouting distance of a Nobel Prize, but a second group was credited with the discovery at the same time, and only the leaders of the two groups got the honor.

There were many back-and-forth dinner invitations. When there was a special event in a family, everyone participated. When we moved into our house, the whole group showed up, each one carrying a garden tool, some of which we still use. They also came to every one of Lore's exhibits, nearby or in New York. I felt quite at home and considered myself to be contributing to the department and its intellectual atmosphere through my teaching, my incipient research activities, and my interest in teaching innovations.

The department had about a dozen faculty members, and it was inevitable that the atmosphere would change as the number grew. The increase (eventually to 60 or 70) led to fragmentation, rivalries, and competition for resources, including office and lab space. Teaching assignments were decided by a committee and were subject to favoritism and manipulation. Cohesiveness and collegiality remained within some of the research groups, but the department became a colder place.

My experience was with nuclear physics and elementary particles, but nothing like that was going on at Rutgers. Later, people came who developed experimental work in both of these fields, but I wasn't interested in doing that. Bernie Serin had been the first Rutgers faculty member I had heard about, and I liked him and his work. I asked him whether I could work in his superconductivity lab. He said, "No, there's nothing left to do and I'm getting out of the field."

This was not the first time that superconductivity was declared dead. At its discovery in The Netherlands in 1911, it was met with great excitement for showing that all electrical resistance disappeared for some materials when they were cooled below what was called their transition temperature. The expectation was that this would lead to much cheaper electrical transmission and to stronger magnets than were known. These hopes were dashed when it was shown that temperatures near that of liquid helium were required and, even then, superconductivity disappeared when a small current was exceeded. Most in the field expected that these limits would soon be overcome, but progress came slowly. There were advances in the succeeding half-century that led to materials with somewhat higher transition temperatures, but the field remained one with great promise and unrealized expectations. It has nevertheless continued to fascinate physicists and to be full of surprises. Before long I found space in Bernie's laboratory.

It took me awhile to understand that the modern professor is not only a teacher and mentor, and a researcher, but also an entrepreneur who juggles a multitude of enterprises and a complicated schedule. Classes and their preparation, research and raising funds for it, organizing the activities of teaching and research assistants, meetings in the department as well as in the wider community of the college and the university, all were part of the job. In my case, I was also developing the radioactivity course and selecting and ordering equipment for the new laboratory.

The job soaked up all my time. But that was only one part of my life. There were also the responsibilities to my family.

BUILDING A HOME

The first challenge was to find a place to live. Later there was the much more demanding transition to life with children.

We had hoped to live near Rutgers and to become part of its community. The area was, however, almost completely built up, and acceptable houses were hard to find. We considered a position for the two of us in one of the dormitories as resident supervisors. That ended when we were shown the split apartment with parts on each side of a dingy hallway. The bedroom was on one side and the bathroom on the other. The arrangement wouldn't have been great even if we hadn't been barely beyond the honeymoon.

For several months we continued to live in Lore's apartment in New York. I took the train to work, and at lunchtime I would wait with a handful of others outside the office of the *New Brunswick Home News*. When the day's papers were brought out, we all scanned the apartment listings to see which one was the most promising—the first person there would get to snap it up. The ad for the one we got said "business couple only." That meant no children. We paid no attention to the supposed limitation and, by spring 1955, we were taking Tommy and a baby carriage up and down the stairs.

It was an upstairs apartment without any air conditioning, and it became very uncomfortable in the summer. We jumped at the chance to spend the summer in the Princeton house of my colleague Ernie Lynton while he and his wife were in Europe. This was not only a great vacation for us, but also led to our owning the building lot where our house still stands.

We walked around the neighborhood of Ernie's house along an empty stretch with only a footpath. One day I went to the town office to ask who owned the land.

The thought of acquiring a house was entirely foreign to Lore. She was more risk averse than I, but I persuaded her that there was no way we could lose, regardless of what happened to my job. In reality, I didn't for a moment consider that there was a possibility I couldn't keep it.

I called up Mr. Cortelyou, the owner, and yes, he would be ready to subdivide the property and put it up for sale. Would we come and meet him in his front yard on the next street, in back of the area that we were looking at?

He had retired from his position in a local bank and was in a wheelchair when we came, waiting with his wife to look us over. We must have passed muster since he called later to say that there would be three lots, one of them six feet wider, and costing 200 dollars more. We thought about the offer for a long time, since even the lower price of $3,200 was a great deal more than we had ever spent on anything. We agreed on one of the smaller lots and went to the ceremonial signing with their lawyer, one to represent us, and Rose Cortelyou signing for her husband. Two years passed before we were ready to take the next step.

Lore had definite ideas of how we were going to live, and I took on her esthetics, which are still part of me. It was going to be a contemporary house, regardless of the neighborhood. At first the lot was empty, except for the poison ivy and honeysuckle, which I worked hard and unsuccessfully to eradicate. And then we found the model for "our" house.

We wanted it to be modern, and not to be in a development

where each house looks just like its neighbors. Nevertheless, we found the one we settled on in a development while we were visiting Lore's parents in a Boston suburb. It was in a group designed by students of Walter Gropius, founder of the Bauhaus, the preeminent modern European school of art and design. They marketed a precut package of the lumber and other building materials. I spoke to Attilio Lattanzio, a contractor who had built the houses of a couple of people in my department. He was called "Ott," not as an abbreviation of his name, but after the baseball star Mel Ott, because he had been a promising player until he had an accident that cost him an eye. He said, "Let's go and look." He picked me up early one morning, and we drove the five hours to get there. He checked the place over and said, "I can build that, but I'm not going to use their lumber." They were not happy with that but, after some negotiating, agreed to sell us the plans.

The house was "post-and-beam" construction without load-bearing walls, and Lore was excited to be able to design the layout. However, putting up the house seemed to take forever because Ott and his crew were in New Brunswick, half an hour away, and our place was not his highest priority. We asked friends to stop by the building site and tell us about progress. Most of the time they said, "No, we didn't see anybody working."

We were excited and talked a lot about "the house." One time when we went to check on progress, Tommy got cranky and said, "I don't want to go to the house, I want to go home." Making the house into a home came gradually. We still have footprints on the kitchen ceiling from the time when kids played on the lumber after it had been left in the rain.

* * * * *

In the meantime we lived in a better apartment in Highland Park, close to the Rutgers campus, this time downstairs, with the landlord's family upstairs. After about two years there, out of the blue, we got an eviction notice. I'm not sure what our transgressions were, but we guessed that the landlady grew jealous when she saw Lore going to New York all dressed up, and she imagined a glamorous life very different from her own.

Our new house was close to being finished. We moved in before we had an occupancy permit and ran a cord through the neighbor's window to provide power. We skimped where we could. There was no attic, no basement, and no garage. I painted the inside. There were no moving expenses, since Ott took our belongings on his truck after we took apart our largest piece, the loom.

The house, with its clean, modern lines, remains a remarkable achievement. In its original design, the 40-by-40-foot space was divided into three equal segments. One was taken up by the living room. We paid for that luxury by having the three small bedrooms, one for us, and one each for the children, uncomfortably close together in the second segment. The third was the kitchen and a utility room with the furnace and washing machine. Some fifteen years later we added a fourth equal segment, but retained the earlier structural elements. The new part includes another bedroom, bathroom, and a study for me. My desk is in front of a large window. The view can lead to contemplation or to distraction. Waves of birds come to the bird feeder; squirrels try to steal from them whatever is edible. Some years ago, a deer was born next door and was left under a bush in front of the window. I thought the mother had abandoned it and tried to give it some milk, but she returned at sundown to take care of her foal, and continued to come back until it could follow her. Yes, I know how destructive they are, but how can you avoid being charmed, especially by a little one? More recently we had a red fox and her litter of four, born in the neighbor's barn. They played under the mother's watchful eye for some weeks before moving on. And then a brown fox with one offspring. There is a wooded area a few minutes from here, and we hope they found a good environment there.

Moving to Princeton meant weakening our ties to Rutgers. The children were the main force making us part of the new community. First, baby carriages and then schools provided immediate bonds.

Two of my fellow graduate students from Columbia lived here. One was Val Fitch, who was now in the Princeton physics department. He remained a friend and was also the only member of that faculty that I knew. John Kessler was at RCA and remained a close friend even after he moved to the University of Arizona. Getting to know others was slow. I made some progress when I started to play recorder and when I joined the small group of Democrats, later to morph into the Princeton Community Democratic Organization.

When the house was built, there were no others in the next two blocks toward town. We were on the outskirts, in our dead-end block across from the school playing field. Since then the commercial center has moved steadily closer. We usually walk the 20 minutes to the downtown area. The Princeton University campus is there, with the richness of its art museum and lecture and concert halls.

THE KATES CRITERION

One of the first houses just beyond the brook was built by our friends Leo and Lee Dratfield. When their daughter Stacy was about to get married in 1968, they set up a tent in their backyard, and we met Lee's sister Ellie Kates, her husband Bob, and their family. It was Bob who introduced me to what I came to call the Kates Criterion.

Bob turned out to be more than a family member and guest. He put his stamp on the wedding, and I had my first experience of his originality and charisma. Stacy was marrying a Latin American, and in his address, Bob not only mentioned that this was a mixed marriage, but added that this is what all marriages are, since they are, after all, between two different people.

He went on to talk about the evolution of the three aspects of their lives, a theme that I have since then used on similar occasions. With their marriage, they were founding a new unit, a couple, acting and working together to build a family and a new life, different and larger than what they were before. At the same time, they would need to remain themselves, as individuals with their own aspirations, strengths, and personalities. Finally, they would be members of the community, as it expands from their families to the neighborhood, the town, to groups and organizations to which they contribute their time, their thoughts, and themselves.

After that first encounter, we saw each other from time to time, and Bob came to play an increasing role in my life as mentor and role model. At the time we met, Bob was professor of geography at Clark University in Worcester, Massachusetts, studying reactions to natural disasters. One was that, after a flood or a volcanic eruption, people tend to move back to where they were before, regardless of their experience with the danger of doing so. This is again a current subject, even more important than it was then. Later he studied the hazards of nuclear electricity generation, a subject about which he remained conflicted.

After 25 years at Clark, he became director of the World Hunger Program at Brown University, whose primary task was to investigate to what extent hunger was the result of scarcity, and how much was caused by policies of marketing, production, and distribution. He left to settle in Maine as an Independent Scholar. Among his many honors, my favorite is that he has been called the father of Sustainability Science. He also became a MacArthur Fellow, a distinction that recognizes unusual originality.

My introduction to the Kates Criterion came when Bob talked about working with Clark physicist Chris Hohenemser on a paper on nuclear hazards. Chris told me about it and used it to illustrate that Bob could be difficult to work with. They were deep in their discussion when Chris said that he had to get back to his lab to check on an experiment. Bob's impatient comment was, "Can't someone else do that?"

When I asked Bob about this incident, he described it as embodying a crucial principle. It goes like this: each one of us has something special, perhaps unique, that we can do, that we can give. Something that others can't do or won't do. It remains for us, and it will not be done otherwise. We have to look for that special activity, or gift, concentrate on it, and give it priority. That is likely to mean cutting down, and perhaps cutting out, activities that may be valuable and important, but that take us away from the task that represents our personal contribution and destiny.

To be aware of it, to look for that uniqueness in yourself that allows you to make a contribution that no one else can or will make, can shape what you do and who you are, and give form and meaning to your life. How far any one of us can go in this direction will vary, but to think about the possibilities and to examine the direction in which your life is moving can be transforming.

The Kates Criterion is Bob's lasting gift to me. I have looked back to see where I have followed Bob's prescription. I can see the themes that have embodied my motivation at different stages, and how they have evolved with my efforts to find the contribution that fulfills the Kates Criterion.

HAVING CHILDREN

When we got married, we knew we wanted children, and the sooner the better. Lore was 32 and I was 28. When there was no sign of pregnancy for some months, she began to take her temperature to check for the time of ovulation. That led one of her friends to say, "If the temperature changes, what are you going to do? Call Peter to come home for lunch?"

After a while Lore had an exuberant pregnancy. She was healthy and radiant. She was also more focused on herself, insisting that this was her time. She did the exercises for a natural delivery and was less welcoming to me. In any case, the presence and participation of a husband in the delivery room was forbidden. I did my best to be supportive, but felt left out.

She was in labor for a long time. Eventually she watched Tommy being born, and later she often talked about how happy she was about that. She wanted to breastfeed him, but that didn't work, in part because of the minimal support from the staff. The obstetrician's remark that she was no *Holstein* didn't help. They wanted to give her something to stop the flow of milk almost right away, and when I tried to interfere to let the process go on naturally, I only succeeded in getting Lore upset.

Tommy was soon an active, lively child, with surprises and

delights for both of us. A woman came in to help around the house, and after a short time Lore started working again. The evenings were ours, and by the time Tommy was in bed, we were played out. My mother had given us a movie camera, and I have a clip that shows the eating, the playing, the reading to him, ending with my total collapse when he was finally in bed. I wanted to participate in every part of raising him and tried to leave work promptly at five, which earned me cold glances from my colleagues who didn't seem to notice that I was the first one there in the morning.

When Tommy was about a year old, Lore began to have severe back troubles that cast in doubt the second pregnancy that I was hoping for. I had been an only child and was determined to have more. After all possible tests, some of which were invasive and unpleasant, the doctors were divided about an operation.

On the morning when it was finally scheduled, the surgeon called to ask me whether I thought she really wanted to go through with it. At that point, and because she had said she couldn't go on living with the pain, I didn't have much choice. As it turned out, the disc operation left her in pretty good shape. She became pregnant again, and watched Naomi being born three years after her brother. Lore was 37, and although having children at a later age is not uncommon today, it was different then. I would have liked to have more, but was very happy with these two. They grew and thrived in their different ways, Tommy a bundle of energy that was not easy to channel, Naomi quiet, sometimes overshadowed.

Lore continued to work, and we were faced with all the attendant sociological obstacles. Competent and reliable help was hard to find, and the cost ate up a substantial fraction of her income. In spite of my goodwill and best efforts, the bulk of the work of caring for the children fell to Lore, and continuing her professional life became more and more difficult.

Society was not geared to helping mothers do anything other than child-rearing, and it doesn't seem that we have progressed much further in the intervening half century. I now look from the vantage point of the much larger resources that are available to me today, and it is easy to forget the limitations of the minimal salary that I had then. Earnings for comparable work are higher now, but so are expenses, and it is not clear that young couples have an easier time today without savings or help from their families.

The sometimes examined life: Bob and Ellie Kates with Mary in Main

PART 5: THE SOMETIMES-EXAMINED LIFE

MORE THAN PHYSICS

I mark the chapters of my life by the major transitions between them. During the earliest one, the upheaval of the forced departure from Vienna in 1938, I was largely a passive participant, with no say in what was happening. I was more active and engaged in adapting to the new culture and way of life during my high school (1939–1941) and college years (1942–1948) in Canada. I took the initiative to study engineering, but it was not really a free choice. It was constrained by the need to gain skills toward a career that would offer assured employment. I knew of no other viable option.

The change to physics after I got the bachelor's degree in 1946 was on a different level. It came at a time when the need for employment was no longer the primary motivation. It seemed to be a continuation of what I had been doing, but to an extent that was not apparent to me at the time, it was a life-changing transition to a different kind of pursuit, and a different culture.

Was the change to physics the destiny that fulfilled the Kates Criterion? I don't think so. Physics framed my life for more than half a century and gave me a great deal of satisfaction. But when I try to think of something that is my own, and goes beyond what others could or would do, I have to look further.

Getting going on a research project in an unfamiliar field for which I had no background turned out to be more difficult than I had anticipated. Bernie suggested an experiment, and I found a graduate student to work with. We had a good start, but mistakes that I might have avoided with more experience or advice caused progress to be slow.

As a result, the research was often frustrating, and without doing so consciously I looked for other activities. Although physics research continued to be my basic work, I now broadened out in a different direction. I found ways to develop my interest in education beyond teaching, and that became the area that opened up my life. It seemed like a natural choice, and I was not aware that it went against the grain, the normal route to advancement and recognition.

The emphasis on research was already strong in the physics department when I came to Rutgers in 1953. Everyone had teaching responsibilities but often looked at them as subsidiary. For me, the balance weighed more heavily in favor of educational activities. I had no experience in any of the research areas of the department, and I had to devote my first years to designing and teaching the course on radioactive materials for which I was hired, in addition to teaching introductory physics courses. In the following years I developed the educational part of my work beyond classroom teaching by meeting with high school physics teachers and by working on course and curriculum development at Rutgers. Balancing the demands of the two parts of my job for time and attention remained a challenge.

From the time when I was still a student, teaching had always come easily to me. I was logical, and once I understood a subject, I could organize it so that it also made sense to others. I could think of myself in the place of the students. I didn't see myself as a human textbook, but rather considered myself a guide through the material, providing the perspective to see what was important, and to distinguish it from the ordinary and routine.

Mathematical development is part of physics, but too often it is seen as all there is, and the difference between the goal and the path is blurred. I remember a student saying, "Physics? It's all math!" That's the way it often looks when class time is filled with mathematical manipulations. For physicists, mathematics is the language we use, but it is not the substance or the goal. The confusion between the two is widespread. The fundamental difference is that in mathematics you can decide on the rules and see where they lead. There can be a connection to the real world, but that is not a requirement. In physics, or any science, you are describing what actually happens, and a statement is only admissible if it accords with observation or experiment. What you do or say is not arbitrary. It must be consonant with nature.

The teacher and the student, the speaker and the listener, are in very different places in the cognitive process, and the connection between them is often remote. I tried to bring something personal to my teaching and establish a connection, even with the large groups that most of my colleagues tried to avoid.

A particularly significant and rewarding part of my work was my contact with high school teachers. It started with my active participation in the New Jersey section of the American Association of Physics Teachers (AAPT) and continued when I started evening courses for them with support from the National Science Foundation for travel and stipends to encourage them to attend. After a while I knew almost every high school physics teacher in the state.

High school courses were widely considered to have stagnated and to be out of touch with modern developments and methods. The most influential reform was the course developed by the *Physical Sciences Study Committee* (PSSC) which was founded in 1956. At Rutgers, Dick Weidner and Duke Sells were among the earliest to hold evening meetings and summer workshops with teachers who then brought this course to their schools.

They also organized the New Jersey section of the AAPT, which provided an important meeting ground. After Duke Sells left the department, I continued his efforts with the group, helping with its program of talks and other educational activities.

Initially I thought the teachers' greatest need was for more knowledge of physics. Many of them had taken only a single introductory physics course in college. Frequently they had started their careers as teachers of chemistry or mathematics. I soon realized that we needed to consider other dimensions as well. The teachers were often creative and imaginative, but the school systems could be stifling and bureaucratic. Most schools had only one physics teacher, so each worked without colleagues in the subject. The courses and programs at Rutgers gave them contact with other physics teachers and provided an intellectually stimulating atmosphere.

The need for connections between high school teachers and colleges led to efforts by the national professional organizations. I was a member of the Education Committee of the American Physical Society when it and the AAPT formed the College–High School Interaction Committee. It brought school and college teachers together at meetings and workshops, often leading to continuing fruitful collaborations. I became the editor of its newsletter, which publicized its aims and activities. There was pressure for me to get involved much more and to participate in the meetings all over the country, but I didn't see how I could do that and continue my work in the department.

There were times when it would have been easy to go in a different direction. An industrial executive once told me, "There are two ways to work: You can work yourself, or you can work through others." He worked through others. I went to Washington twice at the invitation of people at the National Science Foundation to consider one of their "rotating" temporary positions, once in the Division of Materials Research, and another time in the Division of Education. My friends said, "You can't turn that kind of offer down." I saw the airless offices with stacks of papers describing other people's work, and the limited influence of the middle-management jobs, and I recoiled. Those who came back after their stints in Washington became chairs and directors, but that's not what I was after. Working with graduate students also meant working through others, but always with the aim to help them to become independent and to continue on their own.

When I became involved with high schools, I got grants that supported evening and summer courses for teachers, with stipends to encourage them to attend. That's an activity that I stayed with. By the time the AAPT started a program of "high school counselors," it was natural that I would become the regional counselor for New Jersey. Later I participated in a program of cooperation between high schools, colleges, and industry, and I became the editor and main writer of its newsletter. For several years I was an active member of the Committee on Education of the American Physical Society.

I had known that I would not be satisfied being isolated in a laboratory, and these activities allowed me to interact with other people. I was also more active than most in the educational work of the department and the college. I proposed the degrees of Master of Science for Teachers and Master of Arts for Teachers, based on the premise that the usual research-oriented graduate courses were not likely to be helpful for schoolteachers, and that the undergraduate courses that were often not part of their experience were more important. The inclusion of a greater number of undergraduate courses toward a master's degree was accepted by the university over substantial opposition. Bernie and I developed the "general" physics major, less demanding and less mathematical than the usual "professional" major, but good scientific preparation for a variety of curricula and professions—from medicine, law, and business to science writing and science administration.

I became the first undergraduate coordinator of the department. It was going to be called "Undergraduate Director" (as it is now), but I rejected that title. I wasn't going to "direct" anyone. I advised students, helped to organize courses, and was generally a spokesman for undergraduate physics.

As time went by, I taught most of the advanced undergraduate courses and altered them to make them more "physical," i.e., less abstract and mathematical, better motivated, and closer to common experience. The course in Modern Physics (mostly atomic and nuclear physics, and some quantum mechanics) became particularly popular and attracted students from other departments. Some wanted to continue in physics but drew back when other courses turned out to be less inviting.

When I think of contributions that are more personal to me, I think of these interactions with other people, the undergraduate and graduate students, the teachers, and the members of other departments whom I came to know. I also think of the structural teaching innovations to education, the courses and curricula, and finally the textbook that I wrote.

RESEARCH

It was not only a transition time for me, but also for the department and the university. Rutgers was just beginning to shed its image as a small colonial college. Its founding date, 1766, still dominated its seal and flag to commemorate this heritage. There were many steps before Rutgers became the major state university that it is today.

In the physics department, the years after I was hired were characterized by a greatly increased effort to make the department one of the best known in the country. The path toward this goal was seen by the senior staff in increased research achievements. All hiring and promotions were linked to this goal. Duke Sells and I came without any research experience that fit into the new plan. We were the last to be hired without fitting into a particular research area, and we got caught, unprepared, in the drive toward the new orientation.

The criteria for hiring neglected the primary reason for the existence of the university and the source of its economic support: the students. Similarly, my high school activities were tolerated, but not particularly valued. I knew which side my bread was buttered on, so I continued with that part of my work. I saw myself as a bridge between high school teachers and the research community. I organized and went to innumerable meetings that attempted to show that the two groups had common goals and objectives that should draw them closer together.

Meanwhile, Bernie had suggested a research project, showed me some equipment, and then left me alone. I was promoted to assistant professor after the first two years, which gave me a three-year contract. It was renewed once, but then the oligarchs decided that I had not accomplished enough research to merit continued employment.

I had not considered that possibility. I had no warning, no information or mentoring that would have allowed me to understand my situation. My reaction was to become a recluse. I buried myself in the lab and didn't want to speak to anyone. I got angry at Lore when she went to Bernie to try to understand what had happened.

I realized that I had better get something accomplished and some papers written in the time remaining on my contract, regardless of where I might end up. The work on heat conduction had some success that led to better understanding of the fundamental processes. I also made measurements that led to a paper on low-temperature thermometers.

As a result, I had several papers in the works, and Bernie came unexpectedly one day to tell me that I would, after all, be promoted with tenure. It was now 1961 and I was 36 years old.

Henry Torrey said that, even with the promotion, I was unlikely ever to go further and urged me to accept a vacancy at the Rutgers Camden Campus. I saw that as banishment to a more limited environment and did not follow his advice. I wanted to play in the big leagues. The spurt of activity gave me so much momentum that I was promoted to professor after a relatively short time. By the time of my retirement at 74, I had mentored about 20 PhD students, perhaps making

Renata (left) and Erika with me

Elda, Alice, and my grandparents

Helping Nona

Football (soccer) club, with Tommy Czuczka.
Tommy and I in the middle of the first standing row

Part of Elda's Italian family at Dinah's wedding to Ben Zion Aboudi
In 1968. The couple flanked by parents Guido and Fulvia Spiegel,
brother Renato on left

Elda with Swiss Flag, symbol of freedom, on first day out of Austria

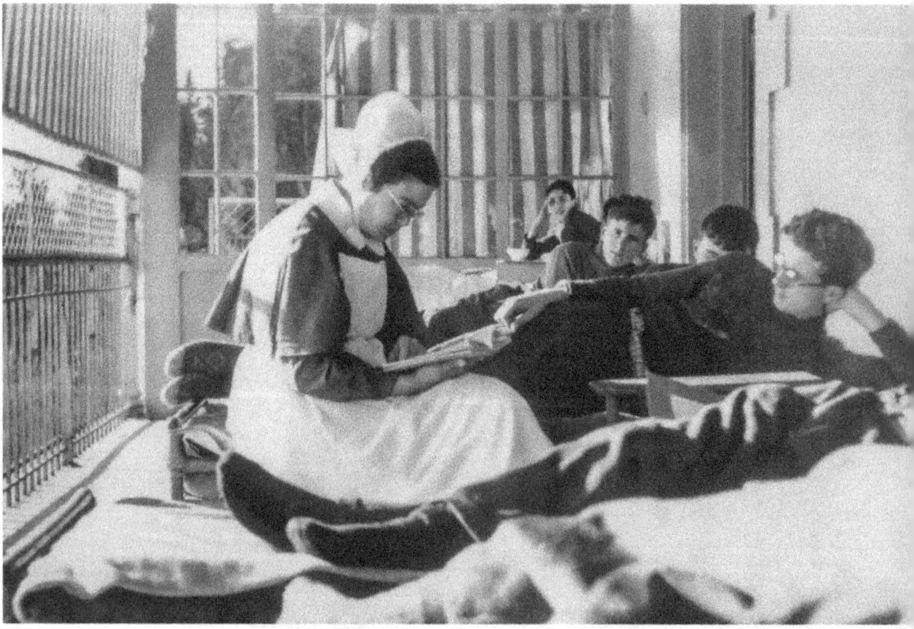

Sister Clara in the Sanatorium des Enfants

On the ship to the new world, 1939

Elda and I came to Canada as farmers. The cow is proof

Early interest in science

COTC (Canadian Officers' Training Corps)

'ith C. S. Wu at the wedding that I conducted for her relative Singteh

Engagement

Wedding day

Lore at her Asheville, NC exhibit with her work and photo as student

Naomi and I playing recorder at Tommy's Bar Mitzvah

Tom reading at his home-made Bar Mitzvah

With class of high school teachers

Peng (now Brian) and Tracie's wedding

Celebrating Millikan medal with Rutgers president Ed Bloustein and members of the physics department

With teachers in Tirupati

Lore and Bela cutting up

Bela in the First World War

Bela holding forth

Naomi watching Lore at the loom

Three generations of Lindenfelds: Tom, Peter, Bela

Tom with Jacque Rubel, parttime "surrogate mother"

Naomi at craft fair

Three generations, a little later: Tom, Sam, Peter

Mary and I, Mount Rainier National Park

Recorder quintet

up for the fact that my contributions to my own thesis had not been distinguished.

The competition between research and teaching activities continued to be part of my life. I am torn when I think whether giving so much of my time to research was the right thing to do, despite the seductive rewards. Should I have followed the example of Duke Sells, who came to the department when I did? He taught a popular graduate course on mathematical physics. He was promoted when I was, but he decided that he would not continue research. He was told that he could then no longer be a member of the Graduate School or teach graduate courses. Not surprisingly, he looked for other opportunities and soon left.

He became *Distinguished Teaching Professor* in the New York State system. This was a prestigious and well-paid position which, however, looked to me to be a dead end. It was in a remote outpost where it was difficult to find students and colleagues, and he was effectively lost to the community. Could I have avoided ending up in a similar professional and personal Siberia?

* * * * *

When I began to work in Bernie's lab, I had no experience with low-temperature measurements and had to learn from scratch. To do anything with superconductivity meant using liquid helium to reach the necessary low temperature. It is normally at four degrees on the scale where room temperature is about 300 and the lowest possible temperature is zero. The grant that gave the faculty extra research time included funds to acquire a helium liquefier. The liquid has to be kept cold in a kind of thermos bottle, and specimens can be cooled with it. Contacts for measurements are made with very thin wires (a few thousandths of an inch in diameter) to minimize heating the specimen. For the same reason the specimen is usually in a vacuum. Each time a wire breaks or gets loose, or there is a leak to the vacuum, the helium and about a week of work are wasted.

My first experiments were not even about superconductivity. Bernie suggested that the quantity called the lattice thermal conductivity of metals was not well known. The largest part of the conduction of heat in metals comes from the movement of electrons, but this additional part is the result of waves (like sound waves) traveling through the lattice made of the atoms of the material.

At about that time, a many-volume *Handbuch der Physik* (Encyclopedia of Physics) came out, representing the latest developments, supposedly the best of what was known. In the article on thermal conductivity, the author described that the lattice conductivity of metals was much smaller than expected, and he attributed that to the presence of a particular kind of imperfection in the crystalline lattice, called dislocations. They were known to be there, but the number that might explain the low thermal conduction was unrealistically large.

Almost any metallurgist could have told me that they had never heard of specimens with as many dislocations as would be required, but the one I consulted was too intent on telling me about his own work to listen to what I was asking him. I was working with graduate student Bill Pennebaker and we wasted a good deal of time trying to see the dislocations with an electron microscope.

A completely different approach led to a resolution of the puzzle. In a normal metal the electrons are the main carriers of heat. They are also obstacles to that other conduction process of waves through the lattice. But below its superconducting transition temperature, the electrons in a metal behave differently from the way they behave in a normal metal.

They cease to be obstacles to the heat conduction process. This was known, but it had not been widely explored. Since lattice imperfections such as dislocations are not affected and stay there regardless, I thought the lattice and electronic components could be separated.

Bernie did not encourage me. "What do you expect to see? What do the leading people in the field say?" I wasn't sure of any of this, but didn't have much doubt that "the leading people" were on the wrong track. We did the experiment and saw the thermal conduction shoot up as the specimen was cooled below the transition to superconductivity. Only the electrons are affected by the transition, and that made it clear that the electrons and not the dislocations were the obstacles that cause the conduction of heat through the lattice to be so low.

The work was published as a *Physical Review Letter*, a short report reserved for significant advances. I eventually had my name on twelve of these.

At physics meetings, I had come to know the author of the theory that I had destroyed. He offered me a job in his department, but by that time I had been promoted and did not want to move. Bernie was surprised that I was on such good terms with him and others in the field. I thought that this was normal and was unaware of the more usual competitive game.

One other early experiment also used thermal conduction and superconductivity. Superconducting specimens in a magnetic field were known to break up into the alternate normal and superconducting regions to what is called the "intermediate state," but only with the field at right angles to the specimen. It was no surprise that the different regions were obstacles to the heat flow and decreased the thermal conduction. That was known to happen when there were any irregularities in the otherwise regular arrangement of the lattice of atoms.

There were no such irregularities known when the field

was parallel to the specimen, where there was no intermediate state, so that the earlier explanation could not hold. To follow up this mysterious result, I proposed the experiment to another graduate student.

For once I had a surefire experiment. We gave nature a clear question and it had to give a definite answer. We mounted the specimen in the apparatus where we could measure its heat conduction, cooled it, and turned on the magnetic field. There were two possibilities. I could have been wrong and nothing much would happen. Anything else would be a surprise and a new discovery that would require a new explanation.

There it was: the specimen's conductivity decreased, indicating obstacles to the heat flow, and an unexpected physics phenomenon.

As we worked more, it turned out that the specimen displayed a new kind of superconductivity, called Type II, that had only recently been discovered. It is idle speculation that we could have done this experiment earlier, and could have been led to Type II superconductivity before it was discovered by entirely different means.

By this time, two additional people were helping to analyze and interpret the experiment, and became coauthors of the two papers that described the results. One was Ernie Lynton; the other was Heinrich ("Heini") Rohrer, who had come to Rutgers as a postdoctoral fellow from Switzerland. He had expected to work with Bernie, who was on leave at that time. He worked with me, and we became friends. We started with a series of measurements that turned out to be less important than I had hoped. The Type II experiment was more interesting, and I was pleased that he would have something good to show for his time at Rutgers.

Shortly after Heini arrived, I went to help him to buy a used car. I was dubious about the reliability of the one he selected, but he was going to need it only for the short distance to the lab during his year's stay.

Two years later he was still at Rutgers and now ready to leave, but he wanted first to see more of America. He and his wife left in the old car, and we got postcards as they made their way to California. They got there and were on the way back when he called to say that the car would go no farther, and they were returning the rest of the way by bus. Their baggage would be delivered on the sidewalk in front of a downtown store in a few days.

I checked the designated spot each day, and soon found their assortment of boxes and suitcases held together with string. I tried to think of a way to get everything into our car and picked up the smallest item, a locked toolbox. To my surprise it was so heavy that I could barely lift it. Lore and I tried to guess what was in it (tools, bricks?) but did not find out until they came back that it contained a specimen of petrified wood that they had acquired on their journey.

Heini went back to Switzerland and a job at the IBM laboratory in Zurich. Not long after, he and a colleague invented and built what they called the "scanning tunneling microscope," the first device that could distinguish ("see") individual atoms. It created a revolution in materials science and earned him a Nobel Prize.

When we later visited them in Switzerland, the petrified wood had a place of honor at their fireplace.

* * * * *

I was happy about those two experiments. They were short, the results were clear and as interesting as I could have hoped. That was not always so. Other measurements often took longer, were more tedious, and did not have such clear results.

When I visited K. C. Mann, my early mentor at UBC, and told him that I was measuring thermal conductivities, he scoffed. "But they've all been measured," was his comment. I explained that the object was not to fill tables and handbooks with numbers on the thermal conductivity of this or that material. This would in any case have been fruitless, since both the heat and the electrical conduction change with the specimen's purity and the physical imperfections of the crystalline atomic lattice. The point was rather to use the motion and properties of the electrons and the lattice waves to probe the inner workings of the material.

I continued with measurements of heat conduction, but I felt under pressure to diversify. Now I think that was unwarranted. I had taken a kind of measurement that had been looked at as uninteresting and old-fashioned, and used it in new ways and for modern insights. I came to know the subject well and had full control over what my students and I were doing. I designed the apparatus, understood what needed to be done and how to analyze the results. The students were apprentices and graduated knowing how to work in a physics laboratory and what it took to do an experiment. They all got jobs that were significant, and sometimes more than that.

This was not headline physics. But it fulfilled some of the features that were important to me. It was firmly down-to-earth, rooted in experiments. It was not highly theoretical or speculative. And it was not done in a large group. The nature of the measurements was not glamorous, mostly of voltages and electrical resistance, as well as the less common ones of temperature and pressure. There was no electronics. I liked that they had to be precise and learned how to make them as well as in the best labs anywhere.

* * * * *

I met Guy Deutscher at a conference in Moscow, when he was looking for a place to spend some time away from his regular position. His family had left Germany when he was very young and he was near the beginning of an academic career in France. He became a regular visitor, and we worked together for many years. I spent a year working in his lab outside Paris, and after he became a professor at Tel Aviv University he invited me there also.

While I was in Paris, we started what is probably the most fundamental experiment that I was ever involved with. The question we wanted to explore was this: as a piece of material is made smaller and smaller, is there a size at which it no longer has the same properties as the bulk material.

We knew a way to make "granular aluminum" by evaporating aluminum in the presence of oxygen and then letting iy settle. The grains are about 300 nanometers across, and the distance between them can be varied by changing the oxygen pressure during the evaporation. At a low pressure, the grains are close to each other, electrons can move freely from grain to grain, and the material acts like a large piece of metallic aluminum. It becomes superconducting at the usual transition temperature, a few degrees above absolute zero. With increasing oxygen pressure during the evaporation, the grains become more and more separated. At first, electrons can "tunnel" from grain to grain, and the material is a semiconductor. For still greater separation, the grains are isolated, and the material is an insulator. As we went through this sequence, we saw the superconductivity decrease, and eventually disappear. In other words, we found that our grains, when they are isolated, are no longer superconducting.

This is the result we were looking for. The separate grains no longer had the property of superconductivity characteristic of bulk aluminum.

The experiment was successfully completed at Rutgers and is described in an informal and readable article in the April 1980 issue of the magazine *The Physics Teacher*, which features one of our illustrations on its cover.[2] It is also on the website firstscience.rutgers.edu.

* * * * *

One summer our conversations led to starting an exploration of collectors of solar energy. We put a glass tube with metal sheets on the roof of the physics building, where it was irradiated by the sun, with the prospect that the energy could be transferred to where it could be used. We made some measurements but, after the summer, Guy left and the experiment was abandoned. I continued to study the energy collection in the laboratory, with various degrees of vacuum in the tube, and showed the different regimes that could be obtained. I built a version with a lamp to irradiate the collector. When it was switched on, the resulting temperature excursion of the collector could be followed on a chart. I submitted it to the *Review of Scientific Instruments* and to an apparatus competition of the AAPT for the following summer's meeting with Guy's name and those of two students who had helped.

At the meeting, I was chatting with Melba Phillips, when she suggested that we go to look at the entries to the competition. Melba was an iconic figure in the community. I knew her from a textbook that I used in my class on electricity and magnetism and as president of the Association, which she had agreed to be at a time when the group needed help.

We walked over and looked at the first-prize winner, a static demonstration of some relations in special relativity. We wandered on to the apparatus that won the second prize, and saw that this was ours. I had programmed the lamp to go on and off, and a trace on the chart followed what happened. Melba looked at the setup and the description and explanation on the table and exclaimed, "Now that's real physics!"

It was a good day.

OXFORD

In 1961 the term of my job security changed from zero to the indefinite future. The previous couple of years had been rough, but my experiments on heat conduction had finally turned out well, and even earned some publicity among the people who cared about this sort of work. It was time for an adventure.

So, when Kurt Mendelssohn, a senior researcher in this field, visited Rutgers and gave a talk, I spoke to him and asked whether I could visit his laboratory at Oxford University in England for the following summer. He said, "Just write to my secretary." That's all the encouragement I needed.

Lore and I were excited about our first trip overseas since leaving Europe. We were returning with the children, who were now four and seven. It turned out to be a time full of new experiences and great contrasts.

The liner *Statendam* provided a week of vacation. We didn't have to worry about food or chores, and the best part was that the children were entertained and taken care of. It was very different from my first ocean voyage in the opposite direction, 23 years earlier. This time there was space, it was fun, we ate good food, and no one was seasick.

Mendelssohn's secretary was very helpful and found a

house for us in Oxford. We would be arriving a few weeks before the owners left on their vacation, and she found a place for us to stay for that time in the village of Eynsham.

We settled down a few doors from the 600-year-old village church and across the way from a house with a thatched roof. Ours stood on the site of Eynsham Abbey, built 1,000 years earlier, with a trapdoor in the floor leading to unknown passages. We were at the center of the village, but only a moment away from open fields. A double-decker bus would take us to Oxford in 20 minutes, again a trip to another world.

By the second day, Tommy was playing football (soccer) with the village children, wearing short pants and looking very much as if he fully belonged. We explored the village and were impressed by the extent of its history, measured in hundreds of years, so different from what we were used to at home. A small grocery store is the only commercial establishment that I remember.

We liked the simple stone church, the first of many that we visited during our stay. Houses were also made of stone, which made them seem much more part of the earth than our wooden structures. The most unusual ones for us were those with thatched roofs. The grass they were made of was pleasing and provided good insulation. I couldn't help wondering how inviting they would be to birds and other animals. I asked, and yes, that was one of the problems of using such a natural material.

We took the bus to Oxford to check on our next destination, a house on a quiet side street. We found our landlady, the wife of a faculty member, stowing away clothes and toys into bulging closets, apologizing for the mess, and promising that all would be in order when we got there. We were happy to see that the house would be easy to take care of, without great pressure to keep it super-organized. It was close to a main street leading to the city center and the colleges and other buildings that make up the university. There was a good bus system, but what I liked best was to get around on the bicycle that came with the house. It had a child's seat that, unlike the ones I knew at home, was attached to the handlebars in front of the rider. It was just right for Naomi, and it allowed me to see her and to talk with her on the way.

Schools were still in session and ready to enroll both children. Tommy attended a regular school close by. Naomi went to a pre-school a little farther away, where I took her on the bicycle. It was a relaxed place, where a mouse behind the radiator did not stir up any great excitement. The physics department was in the Clarendon Laboratory, also not far.

Our time in Eynsham was a transition time. It was very different from home, but it took us no time to get used to it and to feel comfortable. The children were the catalyst that introduced us to other people, and everyone was easy to approach and helpful. I started to spend time at the Clarendon and to make contacts there.

Three physicists had come from Breslau in Germany in 1933, fleeing the Nazis: Franz Simon, Nicholas Kurti, and Kurt Mendelssohn. All three brought their expertise in low-temperature physics. Simon, the senior among them, was widely admired. He became "The Professor," i.e., the head of the department, and also Sir Francis Simon. Sadly, he died soon after, and I didn't get to know him. Mendelssohn had been Simon's student, and I'm told that he expected to succeed him, but he was not so admired, and that didn't happen. I had not realized that he was out of the mainstream at Oxford, and would be at best a marginal host.

In addition to Mendelssohn, what had attracted me to Oxford was that there were two other physicists known for their work on heat conduction, which had become my specialty.

That made for an unusual concentration in this somewhat offbeat field, and I was eager to meet them and to learn more about their work.

They came from different backgrounds and were very different people. Mendelssohn's origin was closest to mine, but I don't think I saw him for more than a few minutes all summer. Harry Rosenberg had been his student. He was a popular lecturer, retaining the accent of his London upbringing. Robert Berman, by contrast, had gone to a "public school," the kind of elite private school whose graduates reflect the speech and bearing of the British upper class. Both were kind and polite and told me a little about their work, but I didn't get to know them more than superficially.

I did get to know some students and others in the Clarendon, but basically, I was on my own. That was not a problem in the rich environment of the university. In addition, our excursions took us into the surrounding area and on some extended trips.

The first journey was to Cambridge, about two hours away. Its physics department was headed by Brian Pippard, whom I had met on one of his visits to Rutgers. He was a bright star over superconductivity and the related universe, imaginative, interesting, inventive, and provocative. I wrote to him, and we made a date. He greeted me with a characteristically edgy, "I won't pretend that I don't have anything else to do," but took me on a tour which made the day more professionally interesting and productive than my entire time in Oxford.

We walked through the Mond Laboratory, which has a circular, open plan unlike the usual block of cubicles. The experimental stations are scattered throughout the small building, and the absence of walls makes interactions and exchanges much more likely than when doors are everywhere. Pippard had many students and collaborators, and on his daily rounds he saw what they were doing, made his comments, and gave them his guidance. It was inspiring to be with him and see him in action. I was introduced to everyone, and later I continued some of the conversations.

After visiting the lab, Pippard walked with me across the lawn. This is a privilege reserved for Fellows and their guests, while others must stay on the paved paths. Altogether it was a very special time for me, with the best possible guide.

One student I met that day was doing an experiment close to that of our work on lattice conductivity. We had quite a bit in common, stayed in touch, and corresponded about it. Pippard said he thought it would be interesting to check the Wiedemann–Franz Law, an old relation between thermal and electric conductivities that had been called into question. When I returned to Rutgers, I pursued this question with a student, and I was pleased that we were able to check the relation with greater precision than had been done previously; we put to rest the doubts that had been raised about it.

* * * * *

Oxford and Cambridge are sometimes talked about as if they were two of a kind and interchangeable, but in appearance and atmosphere they are quite different. Both consist to a large extent of Colleges, separate enclaves with their own students. Each college is governed by its Fellows in a dual, interpenetrating system, of which the university is the other part.

In Oxford, the old colleges are like separate castles, often surrounded by walls with a gate watched by a porter. Visitors are allowed only at certain times. Cambridge seems much more accessible, with wide-open spaces. Oxford has more of a town, with a good deal of commerce and industry. In Cambridge, the university is more dominant.

Britain is known for the importance it gives to rank and class. At Oxford and Cambridge, you're not really part of the elite unless you're the Fellow of a college. In effect the Fellows own the college. There is no board of governors or trustees. Someone may be a professor or have another teaching position, such as reader or lecturer, but that is in the parallel universe of the university. An undergraduate's education is centered in a college and is primarily dependent on his or her tutor, who meets with the student, supervises the student's curriculum and progress, and is often a Fellow of the College. To put the hierarchy into perspective, Mendelssohn was neither a professor nor a Fellow. Pippard was both. For his work on thermal conduction, Robert Berman received a medal, but if you look him up you find out much more about his being the tutor to the more famous physicist Stephen Hawking.

* * * * *

We made many excursions in the area near Oxford called the Cotswolds, with its small villages and their storied charm. We had no car, but buses were quite adequate for the short distances.

At the center of each village is the Anglican stone church, whose unadorned simplicity is its greatest asset. There is usually a pamphlet that describes the building, and we learned to distinguish the architectural features and their history, some going back to Saxon times. We had been told about the "brasses" in the floor or on raised tombs. These are brass plates engraved with stylized pictures, mostly life-sized, of the knights or other important people who are buried there. You could write to the vicar for a date and permission to make rubbings of them, and sometimes your visit would include an invitation to tea with the vicar and his wife. We bought the requisite special paper and charcoal, and we spent many days rubbing brasses. This became a favorite activity the children could join, with the added advantage that it kept us out of the frequent rain. Tourists watched as we worked on our hands and knees; they took us for locals engaged in a peculiar avocation. They asked us what we were doing, expecting us to be experts. When we came back home, we put the rubbings on our walls and had a party to show them off. We gave most of them away, but we still have a few rolled up in a closet.

Rubbings became so popular that the brasses were wearing down, and rubbing them is no longer allowed. In some places copies of the brasses were installed to keep the practice alive. We were fortunate to have been there before that happened.

* * * * *

Longer trips took us to London and Paris for a few days without the children. The two cities were very different, not only from anything we knew, but also from each other. Eating and drinking as tourists, we soon saw the many differences. In Paris, the bistros, cafés, restaurants, and sidewalks in front of them are full of life, gathering places for tourists as well as locals. Looking at people and the passing scene is a major occupation.

In England the nearest equivalent is the pub. The door tends to be almost hidden, so much so that it took us some time to dare open one. There are several small rooms, and we weren't sure where to go or how to behave. In time that became clear, and we got to know their warmth and charm. We found the ones that served "pub food," sandwiches and sausages, most of which we enjoyed, although we learned to avoid some of the specialties. After a few exploratory tastes we stayed away from scotch eggs and pot pies. We got to know the different kinds of beer and which ones were served warm and which cold. There was also alcoholic cider, different from the sweet cider at home. After we got to know our way around, we spent cozy evenings in the pubs. Other good food was not so easy to find. At the time we were there, English food had not yet found its place and was mostly bland. The best restaurants seemed to be Indian and tended to go overboard in the other direction, with spiciness that seared the mouth.

In Paris we didn't look for fancy places to eat. It seemed that you couldn't go far wrong. There were not only bistros and sidewalk cafés, but also street food such as the crêpes that, if you were lucky, were freshly made as you watched. We also liked the spicy, overloaded Tunisian sandwiches. The fruit at the markets and cheeses in small shops were a delight and no burden on our budget.

There were other cultural differences, such as the startling presence in every French hotel bathroom of a bidet. We had to get used to the miniature bathtub that you sit on to wash your backside. Is its presence an indication of the importance given to a part of the anatomy that we are used to hiding and keeping secret? Is it a sign of the proverbial difference in attitudes between the English and the French?

* * * * *

What I liked best in Paris was to walk. Not on the wide avenues, but along the Seine and on the small streets in the Latin Quarter, close to where we stayed. One day I saw a shop window with some intriguing small brass animals. I tried to go in, but it was closed. There was a sign: *Fermeture annuelle*. It was August, the time when everyone who could left the city. I tried again later and saw someone inside who reluctantly opened the door and told me that I had to come back when the shop was open. He told me that the figures were Ashanti gold weights, and when I said we were in Paris only for a short time, he even more reluctantly let me buy two of the delightful pieces, each not much more than an inch long.

The crab and the chicken that I bought became the nucleus of a collection to which I was able to add from time to time. There were other shops in the area with African objects, brought by people who left their African homes when the former French colonies became independent. The Ashanti lived along what was known as the "Gold Coast" of West Africa, now mostly part of Ghana, and traded in the gold dust from the area. Each trader made his own weights using the lost wax process, which allows just one object to be made from each wax model. The ones I like best are the animals, occasionally also human figures. They often illustrate proverbs such as, "You don't have to run to catch a tortoise." They follow traditional patterns, but no two are exactly the same. Their individuality gives each one a personality and an immediate appeal. Other types are purely geometrical, with characteristic designs. Sometimes a nut, or a small animal such as a beetle is sacrificed directly to make a weight in its shape. I also have a brass box used to hold the gold dust, a spoon for it, and a hanging scale. Eventually I had a display case made for them in our living room. Our first time in Paris made us eager to spend more time there.

* * * * *

Back in Oxford, Lore had lunch dates with some faculty wives. I had an invitation from Mendelssohn to a midday meal at the "high table." This was located at the end of the dining hall on a raised platform, where the Fellows and other teaching staff could look down both physically and metaphorically on the main part of the hall while engaging in polite conversation. Mendelssohn took me there, but he did not stay for the meal.

The one dinner invitation was from Martin Wood and his wife. He was a young engineer in the low-temperature lab, working with the existing high-field magnets and making some of the first superconducting magnets. Ever since the discovery of superconductivity in 1911, using the phenomenon to go beyond the limits of iron magnets has been a tantalizing possibility. The strength of iron magnets is limited by the atomic properties of iron. The magnetic field of coils of wire, on the other hand, goes up when the current in the wires is increased. Larger currents cause increasing heat, and that limits the strength of the magnets that can be made this way. Currents in superconducting coils, however, generate no heat. The initial euphoria of this discovery was quashed when it turned out that even small currents destroyed the superconductivity.

By the 1950s new materials had become available, and Martin was using them to make some of the best superconducting magnets. He had shown me his lab, and now I had the chance to talk further with him and to enjoy his and his wife's hospitality. He was founding a company to make magnets, and it later became a great success, making and exporting them all over the world. Some years later, I came across an interview in which he made some generous comments on Simon, Kurti, and Mendelssohn. I wrote to congratulate him and to express my appreciation for what he said.

Some months afterward I had a phone call from his firm, Oxford Instruments: "Sir Martin will be visiting, and he wants to see you." His company had prospered, he was knighted for his entrepreneurship and his contributions to British exports, and there was now a branch and laboratory in New Jersey. We made a date, and he came to my office at Rutgers with his chief engineer. We had an excellent talk, and he was just as open, friendly, and affable as I remembered him. I mentioned his comments about the three refugee physicists. "Oh, you mean the Jews!" Every hair on my body stood up, conditioned by years of aggressive talk about Jews. "I owe them everything," he said. "Whatever I have become and have accomplished is because of them. They gave me a job, taught me, got me started, and supported me." It was a spontaneous and touching statement about people whose background and culture couldn't have been more different from his own.

Later, when I heard about a vacancy at Oxford Instruments, I suggested to one of my students that he apply, without mentioning my acquaintance with Martin. Youzhu Zhang was a hard worker, but I wasn't sure how he would fare under the pressure of producing results in an industrial environment. He had spent two years as a postdoc at City College, now part of the City University of New York. He didn't like the city, and as far as I know, never took advantage of its offerings. He continued to live near New Brunswick, went to New York once or twice each week, and spent the nights sleeping in the lab. He was working for a friend, Myriam Sarachik, who was setting up a lab for experiments that required ultralow temperatures. The work was successful and helped her to become a member of the National Academy of Sciences. Nevertheless, we were both unsure how he would function in the industrial atmosphere.

Youzhu got the job, and we needn't have worried. After some time, he sent us a letter and a photograph from England that showed him with some co-workers in tuxedos as they received a special award for their work on superconducting wires. Today he is retired, but he was still asked to come to the lab each week as a consultant to those who continue his work fabricating wires for a large experimental European installation.

He recently sent me a photo of his wife, their son, the son's wife, and their two small children. It wasn't until he had been working with me for a year or so that Youzhu told me that he had a wife and three-year-old son in China. I helped him to bring them over, and soon the boy, Peng, was standing in our living room with his mother in a little knitted suit that would not be worn by any American child.

Proverbially, it's the Chinese mother who keeps after the children to study, but in this case, I think Youzhu was the tough taskmaster. His wife, Xiaoge, also went to Rutgers and eventually got a PhD in food science. To get a decent job, she denied that she had the degree and worked in the production department of a major pharmaceutical firm until she retired. Peng grew up, learning Chinese on the way, and eventually graduated from Rutgers in engineering. To get a technical job was not so easy for him either, and he found his niche in finance on Wall Street. When he was about to marry his fiancée, Tracy, they asked me to perform the marriage ceremony. I was delighted to do it, this time for a younger generation.

The first time was when one of our students called me to invite us to her wedding. After she talked awhile, it became clear that something else was on her mind. Finally, she came out with it and said, "We'd like you to conduct the wedding." I said, "Sing-Teh, I'm not a priest or a rabbi. That's not something I can do." "Don't worry about that," she answered, "we're already married, but we'd like a ceremony." When I told a friend, he said, "Oh, they just want the video!" And that's what happened.

The whole Rutgers Chinese community came out for her, together with the family of the bridegroom, Paul de Vegvar, descended from a Hungarian-Jewish family. Sing-Teh was related to Chien Shung Wu, the physicist at Columbia who had done the groundbreaking work with beta rays, with whom

I was able to reconnect at the wedding. I worked out a little sermon with Sing-Teh and Paul, and we had a splendid party.

After three such occasions, I thought I was launched on a new career, but that's as far as it went. My little sermons were inspired by my memories of Bob Kates, when he described the widening circles of the couple's new lives.

LORE: STRUGGLES AND PROGRESS

Lore was still very successful in her work and reluctant to give up her career. She began to go to New York less often, and eventually came to a point where she said that she could no longer do it. I thought she would be happy to escape the constant pressure and encouraged her to stop, but it is far from clear that this was the right choice. She went back to work ten years later, but not to the same high-tension, high-power activity with its high professional and personal rewards. She was at the top of her profession, doing some of her best work, and traded that for staying home with the children. She felt great pressure to be at home, and she thought she had to, but the choice came with frustrations and resentment.

She did some weaving, but she found it difficult to concentrate on it in addition to taking care of the children and the household. Eventually she looked for a job again, both for the activity and the additional income. It wasn't easy. She applied for a position at Middlesex County College, where she had a friend in the art department. The college handbook said that previous industrial work would count as professional experience, and I urged her to get documentation of her previous accomplishments. She said she couldn't find anyone who remembered her from that time and didn't give her search the energy that I thought it required.

She always thought that the quality of the product of her work was all that counted, and that others would and should recognize this. She was unprepared for the unfeeling and bureaucratic atmosphere of an organization where formal credentials were more important than actual accomplishment. As a college in the South that admitted Black students, Black Mountain was not accredited. Regardless of BMC's worldwide reputation as an incubator of modern art, her graduation certificate meant nothing to the community college where she applied. She was hired at the lowest possible rank, assistant instructor. Even that was in jeopardy, and after a short time she was told that her appointment would be terminated. The faculty union supported her appeal, and she was allowed to continue on the condition that she get a master's degree. She hated most of what she had to do as having little intellectual content but did get a degree from Rutgers in Creative Arts Education, two years after Tommy's and Naomi's graduation. She was now 61 and was promoted to instructor.

She considered the administration to be rigid and unsupportive, but she liked the students and took enthusiastically to teaching, especially the part based on the weaving workshop that she established. Many students were the first in their families to go to college and had little experience with academic courses, but responded to the hands-on, concrete activities that she presented. It took less than an hour to go to New York, but many of her students had never been there. She opened their eyes, chartering buses to take them to museums.

Jeff Glenn was a student who became a well-known weaver. He dyed his hair blond and moved to San Francisco where he felt that the atmosphere was more welcoming to him and his work. He wrote an article about Lore for the magazine *Fiberarts*, called "Path of Illumination: The Journey of Lore

Kadden Lindenfeld" (1988). The title is taken from work that was inspired by a theater performance designed by Robert Wilson. Sadly, Jeff died early of AIDS.

Except for her time spent with students, Lore worked largely in isolation. When she left after eighteen years, she emptied her desk, and no one so much as said good-bye. She now began to work at home, first on woven wall hangings, and later on pieces that combined stitching and drawing and other innovative fiber techniques. I learned how to make photographic prints on a material that she used, and they became the background for some of her work. She had her work in many group and solo exhibits and was widely admired.[3]

Soon after she left the college, she became a volunteer assistant to Anne Spencer, the curator of ethnology at the Newark Museum, who dealt primarily with African and Native North and South American art. Lore worked on cataloging, photographing, and preparing for exhibits. She particularly admired the openness and inclusiveness of the museum, and that it was a vital part of its multiethnic environment. There were generous appreciation parties, where every staff member was invited, including the elevator operators and the guards. For most of her time there, the director was Mary Sue Sweeney, who came to events with her African-American husband Clement Price, whom I already knew and liked from Rutgers, where he was a professor of history. Lore astonished some of her suburban acquaintances by making the weekly drive of more than an hour to territory that many of them thought alien and dangerous.

Later she became a docent at the Princeton University Art Museum where she was a popular tour guide for fifteen years. She enjoyed the work and the association with other docents but said that she missed the open and inclusive atmosphere of the Newark Museum.

ANOTHER CIVILIZATION

Traveling was built around physics meetings, with my part of the cost covered by my research grants. That was a great fringe benefit. Trips, including those to England, Germany, Israel, and Finland, added a great deal to our lives.

During our earlier year in France, I had been fully occupied, but Lore was at loose ends and felt left out. When we went to Japan a few years later, she made sure to have a program of her own. She was fortunate to make contact with an art school and, in particular, with the woman in charge of the textile program, Fumiko Nakatsu, who became a friend and greatly enriched Lore's stay.

One time, Fumiko took us to her favorite bar for a delightful lunch. "I could never do this if I were married," she said, and explained that she had not been willing to give up her life of independence.

Lore participated in the activities of Fumiko's students, such as a field trip to find indigo leaves which were then used to dye fabric. Fumiko also arranged for Lore to give talks at several colleges. She introduced Lore to the vibrant and very modern textile art scene of Kyoto which had developed far beyond the ancient traditions. We met several of the fiber artists, and later Lore wrote an article about them for *Fiberarts*.

Each of us had our own contacts, and Lore had a better experience than she'd had in France, which made it a more harmonious time for both of us. I knew two physicists in Kyoto. Toshihiko Tsuneto had been one of the earliest visitors to Rutgers. He was now the head of the physics department at Kyoto University. One of Bernie's students, Takao Mizusaki, was a faculty member. Both of them made us feel welcome and helped us in many ways. Takao's wife Faye, whom he had met at Rutgers, had been brought up in Hawaii and was thoroughly American. But she looked Japanese, and that made people, including Takao's family, expect her to act as a traditional Japanese wife. The difference in lifestyle and culture also had an impact on Toshihiko's wife Minako. In America she was adventurous and independent, and I remember asking her what her life would be like after their return to Japan. She shrugged and said it would be Japanese. And indeed, the person we saw, much more subdued, in the kitchen while her husband entertained their guests, was no longer the outgoing and inquisitive Minako we had come to know.

Faye's American upbringing and Takao's time as a Rutgers student caused their lives to be much more informal. The Japanese live in small spaces and social gatherings commonly take place in restaurants. Lore and I felt fortunate when we received an invitation to a meal at Takao and Faye's home with them and their two children. They said it would be sushi. The table was covered with plates of different kinds of seaweed, rice, and varieties of raw and cooked seafood. With minimal instructions we were told to assemble our own combinations, wrapping our choice of ingredients in sheets of seaweed. The results produced in the convivial atmosphere were delicious, and a far cry from the meticulously constructed restaurant sushi that we knew.

By happy accident, friends from home, Martin and Akiko Collcutt, were also in Kyoto while we were there. Martin was a professor of history at Princeton and Akiko a potter whose work we used and cherished. It was through her that Lore made the connection to the art school that was such an important part of her time in Japan.

The Collcutts introduced us to many experiences, the most memorable of which was to accompany them on a visit to a Zen temple headed by Akiko's uncle.

A tall and imposing figure in his robes, the *roshi* (master) welcomed the four of us, and then he turned us over to a young woman, our host for the tea ceremony which formed the first part of the evening. It took place in the temple's teahouse, small, quiet, and intimate, far removed in space and spirit from the busy city. The ceremony itself was very different from the common spectacles that go through the motions for groups of tourists. We had to bend low to enter through the small door and follow our host to our places. She showed us the exquisite pot, the special whisk, the container for the tea leaves, and she prepared the tea in the ritual that required talk be confined to comments on the surroundings and the utensils. Only after drinking the bitter tea was it time to relax from the prescribed formality.

Afterward the guests and disciples assembled for the moon-viewing ceremony facing the open temple wall with the moon in the background. The roshi led the hypnotic chanting, joined by a quite large group of people who seemed familiar with the words and phrases. It was now dark except for the light of the moon as we looked out over the landscape and immersed ourselves in the enchanting ritual.

The ceremony was followed by a vegetarian dinner of many courses, served as we sat on the floor. Lore's posture was evidently not traditional, and one of the young acolytes placed a blanket over her offending legs.

* * * * *

During the previous year, I had made substantial efforts to learn the language. I took a couple of adult school courses, but Akiko's private lessons were both more demanding and more productive. The result was that I was able to make myself understood in shops and restaurants, on buses and trains, and could make reservations on the phone.

The most severe test came after a colleague at a physics meeting told us about a storied but out-of-the-way village for a weekend vacation. He reserved a particular room in a special place for us and apologized that he could get it for only one night, and that we would have to take care of the second. When I went to the tourist desk to make the reservation, the young woman looked at me dubiously and answered, "I think it is only for Japanese." I trotted out a few Japanese phrases and her eyes widened. "I think it will be all right," she said with the characteristic shake of her head from side to side. I had passed.

The room was, in fact, special, with swords and other historic objects from the time of the stories for which the town is known.

The Japanese language was an even greater challenge than I had anticipated. It took me some time to realize that I was learning the language for polite conversation and for shops and markets, but that people actually used an entirely different language when they spoke informally to each other. I already knew that what you say depends on who you are, and to whom you are speaking. Men and women use different words and phrases, and they use them differently depending on the gender of the person they are speaking to. Still more diverse are the differences that depend on the person's social standing. It seemed to me that, with hard work and perhaps another year and total concentration, I might be able to penetrate that barrier and become more fluent, but that was not possible without giving up my regular life. I had to be satisfied with my glimpse of a culture so different from the one I knew.

A PAT ON THE BACK

The university had a higher rank than professor, then called Professor II, which was intended to reflect an international research reputation. By the '70s, I had given papers at international conferences, and I had come to know and sometimes work with colleagues in several countries, and thought I would be a good candidate.

Within the department, however, I was seen primarily as a teacher. I had looked for assignments that others did not line up for, such as the large introductory courses. I felt that I was effective in them and that I could establish rapport with the students even in this challenging setting. Some of my colleagues were happy that a few of us did that, so that they were free to do what they considered more desirable. There was also a faction that thought that those who emphasized teaching did so to the detriment of their research, or even that they were incapable of accomplishing any.

I was surprised when the department chair, who was a friend, and had abandoned his own research activities, asked me not to apply for the promotion. He said it would split the department. I persisted, and when it came to the deciding vote among those who already had the higher rank, just one member of the group voted for me. It was Dick Weidner, who told me what had happened behind closed doors. Dick himself had stopped doing research, and then written a series of successful introductory books.

Faculty members often think that the administration is against them, and that their colleagues are on their side. This is not my experience. Many of my activities had brought me beyond the departmental boundaries. I often found administrators who had a broader view of the goals of the university than some of my colleagues. I learned that your apparent buddy down the hall is the one who is more likely to stab you in the back.

All recommendations went to what was known informally as the "summit committee," the supreme court, known for turning down lots of positive departmental recommendations for promotion. It worked in secret, but I had friends there. It overturned only a vanishingly small number of negative recommendations. Mine was one of those. From 1982 on, I had the higher, but anonymous, rank of "Professor II." Later the title was changed to "Distinguished Professor" as part of an agreement when Rutgers joined the football "Big Ten" conference.

That I should get this high-sounding title thanks to "big football" is ironic, because I was an active member of the *Faculty Alliance for Rutgers* formed to oppose the university's increased participation in large-scale intercollegiate athletics. Our chief instrument was the newsletter of which I was the editor. Our contention was that the supposed financial advantages for the university turned into a steady drain of resources, that the university was being diverted from its educational function, and that the mirage of abundant money led to corruption and turned students into gladiators chasing a rarely realized dream.

In 2007, the founder and chief activist of the group, Bill

Dowling, a professor of English, published a lively memoir, *Confessions of a Spoilsport: My Life and Hard Times Fighting Sports Corruption at an Old Eastern University*. There was substantial support among the faculty, some among students, and resonance at other institutions where big-time sports played an outsized role. At Rutgers, however, successive administrations remained committed to the race to the mirage. A photograph in Dowling's book shows him with history professor John Gillis and me, raising champagne glasses on the evening of the resignation of Rutgers President Francis Lawrence, who had been a particularly strong supporter of the high-cost sports program. We were disappointed when his successor followed the same policy.

Accomplishment should speak for itself, but that's not always how it works. To get promotions, honors, and recognition is largely a political process. Later I got some of these because there were people who went out of their way to nominate me, write supportive letters, and organize others to do so. I am happy about that and grateful to each person and for each of the honors. It is harder to get recognition when you don't blow your own horn, or when eventual success is not obvious, even though you may at that time be in greater need of faith and encouragement.

When I received the Millikan Medal of the American Association of Physics Teachers in 1989, it was a major recognition. I gave a talk at a national meeting, probably to the largest audience I ever addressed, and was asked to adapt it for publication in the *American Journal of Physics*.[4]

I called it "The Einsteinization of Physics," to show how we have hidden behind the popular image of Einstein as someone whose work and thoughts are not understandable by the public. In my talk I reviewed some milestones in the history of physics that were based on experiments that can be easily described. The ones I chose held pitfalls and unexpected turns of interpretation, and raised questions about the way that credit was distributed.

The main part was a plea to make physics more accessible, less remote, and more human. I compared the attitude of physicists to the much more open one of musicians, and of the research physicist to that of the composer. "A jazz musician does not look up to or down on a classical musician ... There are performers, interpreters, critics, teachers, instrument makers, historians—there is even an honored place for the musical amateur. In physics we act as if composing were the only activity worthy of the professional and valued by the community."[5]

I mentioned a textbook on mechanics, famous for not having a single diagram or illustration. As physicists, we have learned to see through the equations to the phenomena that they describe, and to their "music." I showed a picture of the manuscript of a great piece that Beethoven composed when he was so deaf that he could hear it only in his mind. "For most of us the emotional impact comes only with the listening, and it is not so different when we deal with physics." The music can come in many ways. For some it will come in the drama of the persons involved, for some in the historical context of a development or an achievement. It can be in the philosophical structure, in the examination of that which is learned and that which is unsaid, the questions that remain, the answers that are untouched. Certainly also, but sparingly, in the abstract beauty of the equations and the theoretical structure. Most importantly in the direct communion with the phenomena themselves.

"If we can broaden our outlook and methods, perhaps we can become better at including those whom we so often fail to reach: ... those who are turned off by the arrogance of knowledge, those whose expectations have been diminished by failures that were expected of them. If they are not nurtured by us, who will need or want the interpreter and the practitioner? Where will be the pool from which the composer will come? ... I hope we remember that there are many ways to hear the music, many ways to open the ears and minds, to touch the hearts of those who are in our care."

I was thrilled and excited. Many people had words of kindness. It was a recognition of what had not always been valued. I thought my life might change, but the change was in myself, with more confidence in my judgment and a validation of the choices that I had made.

CHANGING TIMES

The university is a complex organism of moving parts, with its departments, colleges, and other units. Each person has a number of contact points, but work and time are primarily defined by the department. When I first joined it, I was an outsider trying to find my way among the duties, the obstacles, and my aspirations.

The teaching was a source of satisfaction, and by the time I was no longer in danger of being fired, I was becoming an insider with a greater array of choices. More than most of my colleagues, I looked for activities that took me to a wider community, but the department was still my primary home.

I was closely involved with everything that went on in the lab. I designed most of the equipment, spent hours soldering tiny wires to specimens, and used computers from the time of machine-language programming and punch-card systems. But by the 1980s, some of the students and postdocs were becoming more familiar with the electronic techniques and computer programs than I was.

During that decade, the department temporarily gave space to a group from *Bellcore*, a successor organization to Bell Labs. They set up a high-power pulsed laser and showed that it could be used to make high-quality thin-film specimens of the still quite new high-temperature superconductors. These are materials that become superconductors when they are cooled with liquid nitrogen, which is very much easier to use and cheaper than the previously necessary liquid helium. When the Bellcore people left after a few years, I inherited that device.

This large piece of equipment with its vacuum pumps and auxiliary hardware filled a laboratory room. When Bellcore left, one of their group was assigned to strip it to its essence, and I found myself staring at a mere skeleton that remained. Clearly, they did not expect it would ever work again.

They had not anticipated the arrival of Sabyasachi Guha, who proved to be a gifted and inventive experimenter. I first heard about Sabya when his wife Lakshmi, a chemistry postdoc, came by my office to say that he was looking for a job. I listened politely but didn't see how I could help. He then came himself, and asked to help in the lab without pay. I was dubious, but he quickly became an active collaborator, and I scrambled to find some support for him. Later he got a regular departmental position which, however, meant that I had to share his services with others. By that time the laser was working, and it became the nucleus of our research program for several years.

The specimens were made, and the measurements done and analyzed by Sabya and Marta Cieplak, a professor in Poland, who had become a steady summer visitor to our lab. I didn't like being part of the group without having my hands on the equipment, but this became more and more the case. I still planned and discussed the work with my students and collaborators, but it became less and less my work. I had projects that I wanted to continue in the former style, but it was hard to do them alone and harder to find help.

Eventually I wanted to have full control over my time and to work on the physics book that had long been on my mind.

There was no longer a mandatory retirement age, but faculty members who retired early routinely got an extra year's salary without duties. I was offered the possibility of continuing to teach part-time, but I turned that down also. Instead, I asked for a two-year position for Marta, which would allow me to withdraw from the lab gradually. I thought that the department would give her a permanent position, but that did not happen, and I retired in 1999.

Was I right to hang on to my research activities as long as I did? I thought that if the grants stopped, I would write and spend more time on the activities related to teaching, and now I think that I might have done so earlier. I continued to straddle the two different environments. I didn't want to give up the research community. It was often difficult, and could be hostile, but it was intellectually challenging. The teaching community was much more welcoming and supportive, but I had to create the challenges myself.

It was rare to be in both communities to the extent that I was, and there was a struggle for my attention between the two, with one or the other winning out at different times. The combination was important to me, and I would have felt a lesser person without both.

Unexpectedly, I found myself in a growth industry. The research grants paid for equipment and supplies and the salaries of graduate students and occasional postdocs. They also paid for trips to meetings and other labs, and for summer salaries that added to my regular salary. When I started out, my fellow graduate students who went to industrial labs were better paid, but that difference did not last. The university grew, and so did the resources available to the department.

* * * * *

An important factor was the activity and strength of the faculty union, the American Association of University Professors, or AAUP.

There were times, especially early on, when the AAUP and a sympathetic administration worked together, often reaching common ground quite informally. Later the relationship became more adversarial and more bureaucratized. I was on the Executive Board of our chapter for many years. The most important work of the group was collective bargaining to seek higher salaries and better working conditions. My main activity was as the long-time chair of "Committee A," the Committee on Academic Freedom and Tenure. This meant that I was the primary advocate for faculty members who were denied promotions and whose jobs were terminated.

My task was to learn about the details of each case, write letters, and appear before deans, boards, and committees. The successes were usually based on combing through the records and finding instances where the administration had not followed its own procedures. Just to say, "This is a good person, and you should keep him or her," was not enough. We were always working on the margin, defending people with flawed records.

I remember one time when I went to the vice-president of the university and told him of a faculty member who was being fired after he had been kept in a minor position far longer than the regulations allowed. He said, "Yes, we should really do something about that," and that took care of it. I don't claim that this success strengthened the faculty member's department, but it was a significant deterrent to further arbitrary action. That kind of informal resolution became impossible in later times.

On another occasion, a dean told me that I could look at my client's personnel file, but not take it out of the office. I made some notes that I then used at a hearing. I was surprised that the dean got very angry, and said he would never again allow that kind of access. In any case, that was another win.

A case that was close to my heart was that of my colleague George Horton. He had been the head of the small physics department at Douglass College (initially called the *New Jersey College for Women*). When the colleges were combined, he became a member of the now unified department but was never quite accepted as a member of the establishment.

He was full of ideas and activities. For a time, he was president of the Rutgers AAUP and instrumental in creating one of its first comprehensive health plans. I was most interested in his educational innovations. He started the *Physics Learning Center* as a place where students could go for help, such as review sessions, student tutors, a library of laboratory experiments, and access to old exams as practice. It was so successful that it was expanded into the "Science Learning Center."

Most importantly, he created courses for students who either had failed one of the regular elementary courses or were in danger of failing. The new "expanded" courses provided more help, more time, more "hand-holding," and a more cooperative atmosphere, while covering the same material. Physics is often used to weed out students; many more now passed and could pursue goals that were previously barred to them.

When I taught one of the expanded courses, the majority of the students were African-American, and the majority of those were women. They had often been discouraged by the unfamiliar course content, lack of preparation, and by teachers with low expectations for them. It was rewarding to see them overcome these artificial barriers on their way to becoming professionals, most often in health-related fields.

George's innovations were widely opposed for lowering

standards, but he was relentless in his advocacy, and his successes were remarkable. He came as professor, and had been at Rutgers for many years, but was not promoted further. Once I held the requisite higher rank, I proposed him for it. The process took three years. The normal sequence let him down. I again tried a back channel, going directly to the vice-president. But this was a different age with greater bureaucracy. He said that we had to follow the proper procedures and I shouldn't even be talking to him about a promotion. George was turned down a second time.

This time the bureaucracy helped. It now included a Review Committee that had the final say. I thought that because of his many other activities, George's research had not been properly considered. I had learned much from George and had become a pretty good advocate myself. George more than deserved the promotion and the recognition that he finally received. Some years later a new administration approved a symposium in his honor. Sadly, I had to organize it as a memorial.

LIVINGSTON COLLEGE

Rutgers University started in 1766 as a colonial college affiliated with the Dutch Reformed Church. Eight years later it had 20 students and two tutors. In 1864 it became a land-grant college and a state institution. By the mid-1950s, Rutgers had grown but continued to preserve the image of a small, elite school that mainly consisted of two components: Rutgers College, for male students only, on one side of the city of New Brunswick, and the New Jersey College for Women on the other. The struggle between the desire to preserve its old image and the pressure to become the large state university that it is today has dominated its history.

In my first years at Rutgers, each college had a dean who ruled with near-absolute power. This was so despite the considerable input and participation of the faculties. At faculty meetings we discussed policies, curricula, and courses, based on the recommendations of faculty committees. Separately, there were committees that made recommendations on promotion and tenure. Members of the faculty often disparaged committees and faculty meetings and saw participation as a burden, but I considered them an important part of my activities. The committees allowed me to get to know colleagues in other departments, and together with the faculty meetings gave me the sense that I was helping to decide the direction of the college. The establishment was rather conservative, but I also found more forward-looking members with whom I identified.

During these early years, Mason Gross was president. He was widely known as the genial and knowledgeable host of a TV quiz show. At Rutgers he was a professor of philosophy, known for his liberal views and non-confrontational stands when students organized sit-ins and demonstrations.

The day-to-day running of the university was largely left to the provost, Richard Schlatter. On the one hand, he was ready to fire people and to institute unpopular policies. He was also an intellectual who sometimes had faculty members to dinner for thoughtful and interesting discussions to which I was occasionally invited.

One of the people who took on a strong role in college affairs in the early '60s was Ernie Lynton, who occupied the office next to mine in the physics department. After a thesis on liquid helium at Yale, Ernie had come to Rutgers the year before I did and joined the low-temperature group, where we became close colleagues. He had already played an important role in our lives by inviting Lore and me to stay in his house during one of our first summers at Rutgers while he and his wife were in Europe.

Ernie's activities caught the attention of Gross and Schlatter, and in 1965 they asked him to establish a new college and to be its dean. Ernie now became Ernest, although he remained Ernie to his former colleagues in the physics department, as he set about creating a new unit of the university. At this point he did something extraordinary and unexpected, even revolutionary that took him far out of his own comfort zone. He decided to create a new kind of college, student-centered in ways that traditional colleges were not. Students would have a say in the governance of the college, and the faculty would play a greater than usual role in teaching and other student-related activities. The students and faculty would represent the diversity of New Jersey's population and be part of the wider community to a greater extent than before. These aims were in strong contrast to custom. Teaching was always taken seriously in the department that I was in, but research accomplishments represented the decisive, and close to the only, criterion for hiring, advancement, and promotion.

Advertisements for the faculty of the new college stated the expectation that applicants would have a strong interest in innovative teaching. This point of view was opposed by some influential faculty members, who said that it was a sure way to create a weak faculty. In their view, research "production" was the only valid criterion. The most vocal persons were the chair of the mathematics department and a member of the physics department long hostile to the efforts of the few of us who tried to institute teaching-related reforms and programs. Their influence was strong enough to cause the mathematics, physics, and chemistry departments to refuse to cooperate, and even to prevent the inclusion of departments in these three disciplines in the college. As a result, the college was born wounded.

Some of the faculty that Ernie hired were later among the most highly valued and respected members of the university. That should not be a surprise. The newly hired faculty members were attracted by the vision of an innovative college which they would help to shape, and which would be open to new and creative interactions with students. They were more likely to have the breadth of interests and knowledge that those who concentrate only on their narrow specialties often lack. I felt excited by the ideas at the basis of the new college. They departed from the old pattern and pointed in a direction that was close to my own interests. Given his new status and responsibilities, Ernie now moved in different circles and became distant from his former colleagues. Nevertheless, he put me on a planning committee for what was now called Livingston College. It was a congenial group that thought carefully about the realization of the new vision.

We were engaged in planning for the kind of college that we would have liked to attend. Was that realistic? Had times not changed? More importantly, what resemblance did today's students have to the students we had been and to the nostalgic and idealistic adults that we were now? The relevance of these questions did not become obvious until the students actually appeared.

Finally, the first class arrived, looking different from the usual, largely White student body. No thought had been given to preparing the ground for the presence of such a wide variety of backgrounds and cultures, notably the large percentage of African-American students. The members of the student body ranged from those who were eager for active personal involvement and the study of social systems, to those who had minimal academic knowledge and experience.

Soon all the students and faculty convened. Together they were to form the governing Assembly of the college. It was one of the first official functions for the new dean, who presided as he had seen it done so often at old college faculty meetings. Reports were accepted, courses were proposed, all as part of a well-known routine. The students only looked on, trying to follow what was going on.

A second meeting soon followed, and Ernie started to go through his paces, following the accustomed rules of order. After a short time, a Black student stood up in the back of the hall and said, "What is all this bullshit?"

At this point the brand-new college came close to sudden

death. A number of students got up to protest the procedure, and this time it was the faculty that was stunned. Some tried to explain what was going on, but the meeting was disintegrating. After a while I got up and tried to explain that there had been a huge effort to create a place where students were much more involved in the decision-making processes than usual, and that Ernie had created a structure that promised to be unusually responsive to students.

After an extensive discussion, it was decided to suspend classes and to spend the next few days considering the future of the college. This was done, and during that time it was agreed to change the governing structure drastically. There would no longer be a single parliamentary entity consisting of faculty and students. Instead, a "faculty chamber" and a "student chamber" would meet and act separately. The result was that governance reverted to the usual old system. Things were decided in faculty meetings just as they had always been. The grand experiment of having faculty and students work together in governing the college was at an end.

I wanted to be part of the college. I believed that something very special was being created. Universities were widely criticized for being impersonal, with admission practices that favored the White elite, and with classes that were often too large. The faculty was seen as too remote, with too little interest in the students who received too little help as they tried to navigate the system. In contrast, Livingston College was a relatively small unit within a large state university, dedicated to working intentionally to counter these trends.

My work and home were in the physics department. This is where my salary came from. Could I abandon this base to become part of Livingston? How would I do that? There was no physics department at Livingston. The faculty formally voted to make me a voting member, and I continued my involvement for some time, but it was peripheral. Ernie was ambivalent about me, and he kept me at arm's length. I had few occasions for any interaction or discussion with him. The one occasion I remember was an eye-opener about my situation as well as about him. He said, "You will never be a real member of the faculty because you are not subject to the system of rewards and punishment of the college." Punishment? I knew that there were sticks and carrots, but I had never heard the practice described so crassly. I should not have been surprised. Teaching assignments, funds for trips and equipment, space for laboratories and offices, and most significantly, promotions and raises, have always reflected the preferences of chairs and other functionaries.

Despite that exchange, I have enormous admiration for what Ernie did. He had the vision that it was possible to build something new and different within the existing structure. It was an entirely new model for a kind of higher education that had not existed but that embodied some of the best ideas and highest hopes and aspirations for a more human and responsive system. A spirit of activism and personal commitment pervaded.

Social concerns were at the core of most of the offerings. At its best, the college and its faculty gave students an excellent education. I could forgive Ernie a lot. I spent a good deal of time explaining and defending him and the college to others.

It turned out that he was not a good administrator. The people he surrounded himself with to run the college were inexperienced and sometimes not on his intellectual level. He tried hard to create an atmosphere of freedom and common decision-making, but the realization of his ideas turned out to be more difficult than he or any of us had anticipated.

Some faculty members devoted themselves completely to the college. They spent such large amounts of time with students outside classes that they could not sustain the effort and burned out. At the other end of the scale were people who took advantage of the system of individual responsibilities and did less than expected. One person lived in another state and came once a week to teach classes. I came to understand that an atmosphere of freedom and flexibility for the students requires the faculty to be doubly dedicated and disciplined.

Student response was similarly variable. The planning committee had in mind well-prepared students committed to their studies and their communities. Only a fraction fit these expectations. Rutgers College represented the status quo, the established system, perhaps not exciting but known and reliable. To a discouraging extent, the students that came to Livingston College were those that could not get into Rutgers College.

A visit to the campus tended to be disappointing. The buildings and grounds were poorly kept up. The bookstore, which we had envisioned as a haven for thought and contemplation, featured textbooks and a few paperbacks, and failed to escape the usual collection of mugs and T-shirts. The administration became increasingly problematic, and dissatisfaction with the college and its dean grew. Ernie resigned in 1973, four years after the entry of the first class.

Livingston continued to exist under less effective and committed management. Its end came gradually, starting in about 1980, when the university began to reorganize in steps that ended the autonomy of the separate colleges. The college deans lost their power and became campus supervisors with none of their earlier control over budgets and academic programs.

Livingston College was an experiment with a transformative potential for new patterns in higher education. One of its lessons is that an idea and a vision are not enough. Support and leadership must exist at all three levels: in the administration of the institution in which the college is embedded, in the college itself, with its faculty and support personnel, and finally, it must come from the people for whom the college exists, the students, their families, and the public. At all levels Livingston was flawed.

Ernie became a vice-president at the University of Massachusetts. I saw him two or three times subsequently, but we did not talk about the earlier times. He was polite but distant. He had moved on. He seemed uninvolved in education reform. My impression was that he had reverted to the person he had been before the creation of Livingston, to the time when there was no hint of the creative spark that powered Livingston College.

There was a small and sad memorial meeting at Rutgers when he died. Few people remained who had known him. The department of jazz studies was one of the innovative successes that Ernie had nurtured and supported. Its former head was invited to come and participate. In his answer he stated the substantial fee that he expected for his appearance. We declined.

I regret that Livingston did not ultimately succeed as a model for a new kind of education. The principles on which it was based remain as relevant and important today as they were then.

PHYSICSEDUCATIONLAND

Education is fragmented. There is no uniformity as we progress through schools, colleges, and a succession of different levels, classes, teachers, and institutions. Most of what happens is less a result of design than of tradition and inertia. My own patchwork education was particularly disjointed, but just how good is the supposedly ideal system that we think of as our model? The rationale for so much of what we put students through is, "it's always been done this way," and "I had to do this, and that's why you have to do it too." Questions about the value of what we do rarely come up.

I would like to spend a little time in Physicseducationland, not so much to talk about my own story as to see whether lessons emerge. Let's look at some questions of sequence and substance. I won't say anything about preschool, elementary school, or middle school, not because I think they're unimportant, but because there is no standard, and teachers can innovate and experiment. There is not yet the grip of the "tyranny of the prerequisite," as we put it in an article in *Physics Today* that described the forced sequence of courses so common in higher education.[6]

For many students, high school is the last time that they encounter physics, or perhaps any science. The physics courses are generally seen as a preparation for college, but their content varies so widely that colleges can't depend on their substance and often pay no attention to them, or even care whether a student has taken physics in high school or not.

Recently I was helping a neighbor's son with his physics homework from the local public school. His textbook, which is also widely used in college courses, is the standard formula-driven fare that invites rote learning and little depth. The largest part is on mechanics and would take up the whole first semester in a college course. Many high school courses barely get beyond this point and pay only minimal attention to what is usually called "modern physics," i.e., the great developments in atomic and nuclear physics after about 1913. This kind of book, and the course that it represents, are among the reasons that physics teaching so often has the reputation of being difficult and remote from real life.

This was the usual high school course all over the country, until a brave and wonderful new course was developed, starting at MIT in 1956. It was named the PSSC course (Physical Sciences Study Committee), and it was going to be a *real* physics course. The people who worked on it were mostly academic physicists who asked themselves what such a course might be like, without any need to follow old patterns. There was inventive and inexpensive newly designed equipment, a series of movies, and a text.

I. I. Rabi, then an elder statesman of physics and an advisor to the working group, said to be sure not to start with mechanics, because the students would be turned off by that right at the beginning. Instead, the book began with a section on "scaling," how size affects properties from the very large to the very small. It is no accident, for example, that our size is smaller than an elephant's and larger than that of a mouse.

One of the most important features was the support system that was established with funds from the National Science Foundation. Newly designed equipment took advantage of modern methods. Tracks with air cushions allowed studies with very low friction. Flash photographs taken at short intervals followed falling objects and other fast motions. Inexpensive optical devices measured the wavelength of light. Teachers were familiarized with the new experiments and ideas in summer courses and workshops, and at meetings during the academic year. They worked with the originators and others from the ranks of the most exciting and innovative educators. These courses and meetings became the spawning ground for a generation of outstanding physics teachers.

Rutgers had a strong PSSC program, organized by Duke Sells and Richard Weidner. I admired the enthusiasm of the group and the strong bonds that were formed among the teachers and between them and my colleagues. One of the participants was David Kutliroff, the physics teacher at the New Brunswick High School. At one point he was part of a joint effort of the U.S. and Indian governments to bring the PSSC and similar programs in other sciences to India. He gave a talk about his experiences in the country and with teaching physics there, and I told him how fascinated I was. He answered, "You can go too!" That seemed impossibly remote, but it did, in fact, happen.

I had a special affection for India from the time when I had Indian friends at International House. Whenever I was asked which country I would most like to visit, I unhesitatingly said India. Now the opportunity was tantalizingly close.

The biggest problem was that our children were seven and ten, and I didn't see how I could desert Lore for more than two months. I told her about the program, and she saw how much it would mean to me to be able to participate. I was grateful for her generosity when she agreed to let me go, and I was soon on a plane to Delhi, studying the PSSC text.

* * * * *

Once we landed in Delhi, an efficient Indian assistant whisked our small group of Americans through customs by bullying an assortment of officials. We got to the hotel where there were going to be two days of orientation sessions. My more experienced friends had suggested that I skip them, and so, after registering, three of us were on the way to *Chandni Chowk*, the main street of Old Delhi.

We wandered on, overwhelmed by the variety and multitude of sense impressions. In front of the shops, on the sidewalks and on the street an unending line of people sat next to their wares, shouting to the passersby, bargaining with them, or talking with their neighbors or their families which in many cases surrounded them. Off the street are narrow alleys. The shops are holes in the walls. In some, barbers cut customers' hair (always including the hair on their chests), in others food is prepared: small dumplings dipped in butter, syrupy pretzel-like concoctions, or the famous pan—a large leaf smeared with spices, jams, pastes, covered with an almost infinitely thin sheet of pure silver, and rolled up. One man rolled up a particularly artful pan, offered it to us, and refused payment, only smiling proudly that he could offer us a gift.

There were outstretched hands too, there were diseases, there was poverty. But whether it was my mood or not, I found that the vitality, the variety of life, the strength of the colors, the sounds and the smells, made the greater impression on me. I found the scene exhilarating.

I went back twice more to Chandni Chowk and felt the

same way each time. I visited no museums, tombs, mosques, or temples. Some of my colleagues were aghast that I passed up visits to the Taj Mahal and the other tourist sights. But I felt that even if I saw nothing else, the journey would have been worthwhile.

* * * * *

In Delhi, I met Bryan Swan, a Chicago high school teacher who was to be my teammate at Sri Venkateswara University in Tirupati, partway between Madras and Bangalore. Before getting to our destination, we had a couple of days in Madras (now called Chennai) because the university was closed because of protests against the adoption of Hindi as the national language. The ruling was accepted in the North where Hindi is the basis for what is spoken, but not in the South where the languages are more diverse, and English has been a unifying force.

We were in our hotel room, trying to learn a few words of Tamil, the local language, from material that we had been given at the American consulate. That did not turn out to be helpful since Tirupati is in the neighboring province of Andhra Pradesh, where the language is Telugu.

On the first afternoon we had the unannounced visit of Professor Bhimasenachar, the head of the physics department where we were headed, and our host there. His message was simple: "This PSSC, are we going to treat it as a religion, or is there a chance that we can also do something else? What these people need is a workshop where they learn how to build things."

Since we were there to teach the PSSC course, we saw this as an assault on our mission. We rejected his suggestion, and when we finally got going there was no deviation from the original plan. As is usually true for those involved with a new program, we thought of ourselves as missionaries ready to defend the purity of what we were doing against distortion and dilution.

Today I would be more curious and ask ourselves what would be best for the participants, a wonderful group of teachers from two Indian provinces, some from cities, some from low resource rural schools. "Book learning" is what they were used to; hands-on experience building simple equipment would have been very helpful to them. We decided instead that what they needed was "real physics" as that's what we saw as the purpose and substance of the PSSC program.

As I look back, I see what we were doing in India had some of the same flaws that caused the PSSC course gradually to disappear at home. The course was physics at its best, as it had not been seen in high schools. It was developed by an outstanding group of people, led by physicists at our best institutions. They produced a revolutionary course. But when it came time for it to live on its own, it did not survive. Why did the PSSC course disappear? It was a challenge for the teachers, who came to it familiar only with the courses that had been part of their own education and that had been around for decades. That's why the support system with its summer courses and winter meetings was so essential. As soon as the PSSC course was considered ready to stand on its own feet, the support was phased out. The recruiting of new teachers, the involvement of university faculty members, and the enthusiasm that had been generated disappeared also. The book and the program changed, but not for the better. The introductory chapter on scaling was eliminated, and the emphasis on mathematical and abstract examples was increased. The level proved to be unrealistic. It became a course for elite students while the previous unreformed and old-fashioned courses continued for the majority.

The course is today only memory and history. But it was seminal and had a great influence on the courses that succeeded it. The effects of the revolution that it represented remain. Many of the innovations in lab equipment and methods are used in courses today. The PSSC course was made possible by major government grants, but its success came from the ideas and collaboration of inventive and dedicated people from universities, high schools, government, and industry.

My time with the PSSC course came at its height. I think of my involvement with it and being in India as one of the transformative experiences of my life. I felt that we were making important contributions.[7]

WRITING A BOOK

In colleges the introductory physics course has been taught largely unchanged for many decades, and except for brave experiments like PSSC, high schools have mimicked these courses. What are students going to do when they get to college? Take the same kind of course again? Will it be better, more sophisticated? Will they learn more? Or will they be so bored (as I was in this situation) that they stop paying attention altogether?

There are courses both in high schools and in colleges that don't try to follow the rigorous and mainly mathematical pattern thought to give the proper background for a science career. They are often called "conceptual," and tend to be looked down on as not being "real" physics; but because they concentrate on ideas rather than math, they often give a better view of physics and more generally of science. An early text that followed this less rigorous path was called *Physics for Poets*.[8] Its audience was small (it turns out that there are not many poets who want to study physics), but the title continues to be used generically (not always approvingly) for courses that de-emphasize mathematics.

* * * * *

My interest in these questions is more than cursory. At first, I had worked on a physics textbook book alone, but found that difficult. I then asked Suzanne White Brahmia to work with me; I did almost all of the writing and we went over everything and discussed it in detail. We tried to imagine what a first college course should be like, and to describe it in a book. She contributed many ideas, and the collaboration was fruitful. The book, *Physics, The First Science*, was published by Rutgers University Press in 2011.[9]

In our first exuberant public statements we said, "Physics teaching will never be the same." That's not the way it worked out. We know some of the reasons: The book looks easier than it is; it requires a substantial effort; it did not go through a period of tryouts in classes other than ours; and it was barely advertised or promoted. It may also be that the era of the old textbook is over. My grandson tells me that his generation doesn't need to memorize, or apparently even know anything anymore—you can get it all instantly on the internet. Does that include understanding, being able to think, to analyze, and to use knowledge?

I see physics as a humanistic subject, and the development of physics as an essential part of intellectual history. This perspective provided both the motivation for looking at the subject anew and the thrust of our book's narrative. The text does not ignore the fact that physics is the foundation of our technical civilization, and that its concepts are, more often than not, regarded as remote and inaccessible. The book aims to demystify the subject, to use straightforward language, and to use mathematics to simplify rather than to obscure.

We tried to write as if there had never been a physics text before. Our aim was to present a coherent picture of the world rather than a collection of miscellaneous facts and factoids. The goal was to illuminate nature in a way that enabled students to see more in it than they had before. Mathematics is an important part of the language of physics and, in our book, we do not avoid all mathematical developments. But we make it part of the narrative, not set off in boxes with formulas to memorize.

We paid no attention to speculation; we left out the "gee-whiz physics" and the sensationalism. This goes counter to the current trend that attracts people to phenomena and topics that are strange and far away from experience. We stayed with what touches our lives. For each part and for each phenomenon we asked ourselves, "What do we want to say? Is this important enough to include? What is essential, and what can we say to make it clear and part of the story?"

The book contains more about concepts than is usual, more physics than much thicker books, even while it does not skimp on the mathematics. One of our highest rewards was that it got the three really good reviews in the major relevant physics journals.[10]

There is a small wave of books based on *Physics Education Research* (PER). This is a relatively new discipline based on the premise that the effectiveness of teaching needs to be ascertained by research, using means such as tests, interviews, and surveys with statistical analysis, rather than the intuition, imitation, tradition, or the ego of the teacher. PER emphasizes that it is not enough for the student to feel good about the teacher and, more important, not enough for the teacher to feel good about himself or herself. There has to be reproducible evidence that the students have actually learned the material. A conclusion is that teaching requires the active participation of the student: passive listening to lectures has little effect. PER has had substantial success and is increasingly influencing physics teaching and learning.

PER focuses on how to reach students so that they learn,

understand the material, and retain it. It pays little attention to the choice of subject matter, which most often follows tradition. Our book departs from the mainstream. In each section we asked ourselves, "Is this necessary?" Occasionally, we put in something that's just interesting or fun. The result is a book less than half the size and weight of the usual textbook with about a third of the usual number of pages devoted to mechanics. The outline is close to what you find in a traditional text, but what we do is quite different.

Readers have remarked on our innovative introduction to quantum mechanics, the subject that is the basis of all modern understanding of the structure of matter. In most elementary courses it is barely mentioned, or else alluded to only superficially as an unexpected revolution. We show that it came organically out of historical and intellectual progression, and is rooted in earlier developments.

Although quantum mechanics was developed in 1925 and underlies some of the most important technical developments that are part of our lives, it has only, to a minor extent, entered public consciousness. We think we have gone far to make the subject and its concepts more widely accessible.

* * * * *

Even a fairly comprehensive elementary course can hardly be more than an introduction. So, when do we get to the real thing? Where do we get closer to knowledge of the subject? Although they don't always do it, the more advanced undergraduate courses can provide that more detailed and usable knowledge. My own experience as a student is not a good guide, but I have taught enough to learn how much can be done. I have endeavored to present each subject in its historical and scientific context, describe its motivation and aims, and give an account of its basic principles, achievements, and applications.

Sometimes when I was dissatisfied with my undergraduate classes, I thought that more complete and satisfactory knowledge would come in graduate courses. That is rarely what happens. Graduate courses stress more complicated mathematical techniques but not many new ideas or principles. Some of the traditionally taught mathematical parts have become obsolete with the development of computers, but the curricula don't easily catch up.

The graduate curriculum often includes an oral comprehensive exam. Not surprisingly, it is dreaded by the students and generally found unsatisfactory by the faculty. It is usually unbounded. The examiners can ask anything they like, and the student is supposed to be ready with answers for everything. It is often said that they should"think like a physicist." But faculty members tend to draw on problems from the storehouse that they are familiar with, and I have too often seen them struggle with questions that are new to them.

Students tend to concentrate on preparing for complicated questions and are less prepared to answer those that deal with the fundamentals. I remember one final doctoral exam where I was rooting for the student when an examiner asked an elementary question about atomic physics. I was about to relax when, to my disappointment, the student ignored the obvious simple answer and tried something more abstract and difficult that got him stuck in a morass.

One of my more successful proposals to the department was to limit the material for the exam for a master's degree to knowledge that is found in a good introductory book. The courses that use these books tend to deal with the material only superficially, but the books, including ours, provide much more. This was a way both to limit the amount of preparation and to encourage students to focus their attention on more interesting, somewhat advanced and subtle topics.

* * * * *

Do we really need teachers? Aren't books enough? And do we need books now that we have the internet? A wave of "*self-paced*" courses became popular for a while (was it in the 1960s?). Students were given books and assignments and the teacher became a "resource person." One of my friends visited a major university where a course that used to be held in a lecture hall had been replaced by sessions in a large room where students worked individually, and the instructor and the teaching assistants were in phone booth-like structures scattered throughout the room, waiting to be asked for explanations and answers to problems.

At one time the dean of the School of Education asked me to help find a faculty member to teach Science Education, and one prominent person said he would accept if we provided a whole school organized on the self-paced principle. That did not happen. In fact, the movement toward self-paced courses soon died. It turned out that neither the students nor the instructors liked the idea. The teachers felt underused and more surprisingly, the students preferred the much-maligned old-fashioned classes. They wanted and needed the contact with teachers, the perspective, and the experience that only a human being can provide. They needed the pacing and the scheduling that were now left largely up to them. Some students liked the responsibility and could meet it, but they were much rarer than expected. The system of which so much had been expected soon disappeared.

Experiments with methods that involve computers are proliferating. Some are motivated by economic concerns. In computer-based courses a single instructor can be assigned to a large number of students who, supposedly, need nothing but a screen and a chair. Unsurprisingly, it turns out that they also need the motivation and the will to participate and keep up.

Other experiments have been forced by the isolation demanded by the virus-based pandemic. The changes are so widespread and fundamental that it seems unlikely we will fully return to the former methods. The students need to learn to think about the subject matter independently. The instructors have to adapt and find ways to make themselves more than a face on a screen. Success seems to depend on the extent to which personal interactions that characterize the best classroom teaching can happen in this very different setting.

ON RETIREMENT, 1999

This is the year of two blue moons.
Twice this time the moon shines bright
twice in a row before the month is out.

Does it, the sun, the stars
determine what we do?
Not likely. Still, they do provide
that cyclic certainty
the background to our lives
as they evolve
this moment to the next
ever new never known
until it slips
through present into past.

It is now time to change
the cycle anchored for so long
returning after each excursion
in time and space
to action and allegiance
to this point of equilibrium
and stability.

There have been joys
there have been friends
young faces lighting up
in sudden recognition and response.

Struggles
more often than not
choices
not always wise
the path
only sometimes straight.

Insights
slowly fought for,
glimpses
of the promised land.

So much not done.
Is there still time?
I think of one who quit
after long years with what was not his first priority
saying now I will do what I had to put aside
but that is not what happened
and the friend who said
if there is something that you want to do
don't wait.

Will your lifestyle change they asked
and seemed surprised
when I said yes.

I look for times when call and pressure
come only from inside myself.

Time to look inward
to children, wife, family
and self,
to dream, to read, to write,
and outward
to the beauty
and the strains and battles of the world.

Explore behind doors that had been closed
travel to places that we know
and some that will be new
visit those who were remote too long.

A new life yes
but one where friends
and activities of earlier days
will still be there.

It may be good-bye to the shackles of the schedule
but it's hello to you.
Don't go away.
I am still here.

Family: Naomi celebrating her 60th birthday with friend Tita Hilsdon
Naomi's husband Michael is lighting the candle.

PART 6: FAMILY

GROWTH AND DEVELOPMENT

Tommy was a whirlwind from the start. It was a stormy night when we drove to the hospital, which Lore would later describe as a fit beginning. After we moved into our new house in Princeton, our first improvement was to put in a solid door between the bedroom area and the rest of the house, but Tommy wouldn't go to sleep when this door was closed. He didn't want to miss any of what was going on. One day when he was perhaps three, a class lined up in the school playing field across the street and he ran over and lined up with the others. I hated to have to tell him that they couldn't include him.

He was very much part of our life. We talked to him, read to him, took him to parks, picnics, and most places that we went. He soaked up whatever was happening, and he wanted to be part of it all. It should not have been a surprise that when Naomi was born three years later, she was very different. She was quiet, presumably reacting against the commotion that Tommy produced, and the talky, busy atmosphere in the house. It took her awhile to start to speak. She didn't say very much, but when she did, she thought about it carefully. Early on we visited my mother in Vancouver and Naomi saw the beach and the ocean for the first time. She sat on the sand, looking out for a long time. Finally, she turned to Lore and said, "Mommy, lots of water!"

What I had learned from my psychiatrist mother was that each child and person is shaped by the experiences and impressions that he or she is subjected to. Her course on family dynamics was about the different patterns of influence on first children, second children, parents, and so on. But I don't remember any mention that each child comes with a huge amount already built-in. That was new to us. We had to get used to the fact that we had two children with very different personalities, reactions, and eventually aspirations. We followed the debates and controversies about how much of a person's personality is inherited and how much is shaped by influences and experiences. Today we know that each part plays a determining role.

Naomi was quiet, thoughtful, and kind from the beginning and has remained so. During her early life we wondered sometimes whether she would navigate the world successfully. School, with its sometimes rigorous and often irrational demands, was an obstacle. When Naomi got to high school, a new program called the Learning Community had just been established in the local school system. A place was set aside for a group of teachers and students as a school within the school. There was more attention to individual development and support, sometimes outside the normal routine. It fostered a strong feeling of community and common purpose and emphasized cooperation over competition.

For Naomi this was a good environment. She was always more comfortable with visual and tactile elements than with those that were abstract and form the bulk of the usual curriculum. The highly structured subjects, such as math and science, did not come easily for her. She felt at home in the supportive atmosphere of the Learning Community, where she had more protection than in the usual everyone-for-himself (or herself). She started drawing with confidence and imagination, and she took an early ceramics class. She gradually overcame her shyness and made close friends.

The Learning Community no longer exists. It required extra personal involvement and commitment from the teachers and a sustained support structure. It is rare, even for successful innovations, to survive without the presence and enthusiasm of the founders. We were happy that the Learning Community was there for Naomi. She says that it saved her.

Naomi was twelve when I had a sabbatical and all four of us spent a year in Paris. I learned about the French school system of that time. The principle seemed to be that you went as far as you could in increasingly advanced schools, took the required tests as you went along, and were eventually sifted out. To a large extent, the point at which this happens determines your life and standing from then on. The system is quite rigid, with little room for deviations. The school program and exams are nationally determined, so that on a given day, no matter where you are, what goes on in a classroom is the same in all classrooms at that level. In the normal course of events, you can go to university after passing the *baccalauréat*, a stiff exam much like the one that my parents underwent. Unique to France, there is, in addition, the parallel system of the *grandes écoles*, which was instituted around 1800 to create an elite civil service. They include the famous École Normale and the École des Sciences Politiques, and some that are less well known, such as the École des Mines. The biggest hurdle is to get in and would-be students attend special cram schools to prepare for the competitive entrance exams.

The social revolution of 1968 was supposed to bring about changes, including better access to universities and less centralized control over admissions, curriculum, employment, and advancement. I saw some of that in the laboratory where I worked, which was associated with the University of

Paris. A lab council now included students and technicians. Unsurprisingly, the *mandarins*, the circle of insiders at the top, derisively named after the early ruling bureaucrats in China, continued to make the important decisions, such as those on budget and personnel.

Tommy and Naomi started in the *école bilingue* where both English and French were used. We thought it would be just right for them, tailor-made for international students. Instead, at the end of the first semester, they revolted and announced that they did not want to continue. It was too ordinary and they didn't feel that they were learning anything about France. We found a French school for Naomi with the kind of encouraging atmosphere that she thrived in. It was outside the city, and she had to take a bus and then a train. She quickly became comfortable in the school and with the ride. Once, when she missed her train stop, she found her way back without difficulty. The school arranged for classmates to come to our apartment once a week to help her. I remember one who read *Snoopy* comics in French with her. A lot of laughter came from the room where the two worked together. Altogether the year was a very positive experience for her.

As the children grew up, it became clear that they were going to go in very different directions from each other and from me. Understandably, they were going to avoid competing with my kind of activity. Although Naomi did not exactly follow in Lore's footsteps, her work was close to her mother's in spirit. She did a lot of drawing and early on developed a characteristic and individual style. Her progress through school was steady, and she knew that she wanted to go to a college that would allow her to develop her artistic skills, which were direct and manual, rather than abstract.

Tommy's progress was much more erratic. His first year in

Princeton High School was at a time of widespread political and social protests. It was 1968, the Vietnam War had started, and young people were questioning established ways. Tommy participated in sit-ins more than in schoolwork. He was uninterested in most classes, and his results reflected that. At the end of the year, he failed all his courses.

The next year was our year in France, and after the first semester in the école bilingue, he enrolled in a French *lycée*. He was obviously unprepared for the rigorous curriculum, and barely able to make out what was happening. It was no surprise that the highly structured program left him out.

That does not mean that the time was lost. He learned a good deal of French, spent time playing chess, made friends, and went on political demonstrations with them. This was just after the social upheavals of 1968, and students were still protesting by blocking traffic on the main boulevards. More than once, we were startled as we looked out the window to see Tommy among them, sitting down in the middle of the street.

It was time for a family conference. "You can go back home and waste your time, just like last year. But if you want to change that, we will help you find a different school." He understood that he was at a crossroad. We studied the possibilities together, and he applied to Simon's Rock, then in Great Barrington, Massachusetts, whose four-year curriculum bridged high school and college. The title of his application essay was, "Why All Schools Should be Abolished." We tried to tell him that he was, after all, applying to a school, but he was not deterred.

When summer came, we were not ready to leave France, but Tommy pressed us to let him go back alone. We balked and came to an impasse, when he came up with a solution: "Let me go and stay with Jacque." Jacque Rubel had become a friend after she took an adult-school weaving course with Lore. She had a summer camp for children along the Millstone River about 20 minutes north of Princeton, called CAPA, Camp for Creative and Performing Arts. She had the ideal qualities for running the camp and for Tommy: firmness and authority together with warmth and acceptance. We knew that Tommy would be in good hands. Even better, she gave him the responsibility of working with younger children. She became a surrogate mother for him, someone to guide him without the stresses of his relation to his parents.

When we got back to the States in the fall, we drove to Simon's Rock for an interview. The admissions officer greeted us and took Tommy into her office. After a while they came back and we were surprised when she started to say goodbye. "Don't you want to speak to us?" "No," she said, "we knew his parents hadn't written his essay." They accepted him, and the school did, in fact, change his life and give him an education. Classes were small, discussion was encouraged, and social commitment was emphasized.

Tommy stayed for two years at Simon's Rock, but he came home without a high school diploma. He drifted with no apparent purpose, and after a while we told him that we would pay for further school or college, but that otherwise we would expect him to become independent and move out. He started by volunteering in a halfway house for transitioning prisoners of Trenton State Prison, which led to his becoming the resident assistant manager. He learned to cook for 20 people and attended their therapy sessions. From time to time, inmates were released in his custody for holidays and family celebrations, and he accompanied them to their homes and participated with them.

The prisoners were there for serious crimes, and this was a substantial responsibility. Tommy, not yet 20, got to know them personally and established rapport with them and their families. This is an example of the people skills that have marked his life.

After two years at the halfway house, Tommy became a volunteer on political campaigns. While he was with the campaign of Morris Udall for President in 1976, one of his fellow workers asked him to take her place as a research assistant at Princeton University's School for Public and International Affairs. That went well enough, but the faculty members that he worked for soon found out that he was not a graduate student, nor, in fact, any kind of student, and had not even graduated from high school. They told him that he could continue as an assistant, but he would never get further without more education.

Tommy understood that and said he would "consider" being a student at Princeton. I told him what I thought his chances were to get in (zero), and I suggested Rutgers. He paid no attention to my advice and embarked on a campaign to support his application. Several people wrote letters of support, and three Princeton faculty members recommended to the admissions office that he be admitted in spite of his nonexistent academic record. As fluky, unexpected, and unpredictable as it was, that's what happened.

Tommy's favorite subject at Princeton seemed to be independent study. This included time away at *Delancey Stree*t, a residential program in California for recovering addicts, where he lived for a semester. The participants had to work, and Tommy joined them at their moving company. He called one time and said they were just moving a piano upstairs. Lore and I looked at each other. "Is this what we're paying Princeton tuition for?" He based his senior thesis on his experiences and was awarded the school's prize for the year's best thesis.

The graduation from Princeton at 25 changed the path to the rest of his life and shaped his subsequent progress.

CONFLICTS AND RESOLUTION

By the middle '60s, the tensions between Lore and me became more difficult for both of us. For one, we had different attitudes toward the children. When they were younger, our daily lives and our recreations were built around them. We read to them, we talked to them, and took them to parks and on hikes. We put on puppet shows on their birthdays and looked for family activities that included them and often their friends as well.

That doesn't mean that we had an easy time with them. Lore insisted that we had to be consistent. When Naomi asked to go to a concert in Newark and we thought it might be dangerous, we said no. When she came back with "all my friends are going," I was willing to negotiate. To Lore, I was a traitor who failed to support her. To me, she was harsh and rigid. The children soon learned to take advantage of our differences.

Money was another source of conflict. From the beginning, we had a common bank account, and I had to have Lore's agreement for all expenditures. She was willing enough to spend money for what she considered important, such as the children's education and family vacations, but she hated to see me spend money in ways that she considered frivolous.

I had to negotiate for all but necessities, including the occasional food luxuries, useless decorative items, or expenditures for hobbies such as my coin collection. Even money for charities did not make her list. During the first years we had to skimp because of my small salary, but her attitude never changed. When we eventually accumulated a cushion, her mantra remained, "When you really need it, you never have enough."

A restriction I found particularly confining was that she didn't want me to go to evening meetings. I had become active in the Democratic Party, becoming a founding member of the Princeton Community Democratic Organization (PCDO). Political engagement has always been important to me, and when we moved to Princeton, I joined the small band of Democrats who met in the firehouse above the fire trucks with a group of old-timers known as the Firehouse Gang. Some of us were dismayed with the lack of intellectual activity and the seeming impossibility of dislodging the town's uniformly Republican officeholders.

We asked Mel Gottlieb, an imposing and charismatic figure who was the head of the Princeton Plasma Physics Laboratory at the time, to take charge of a new group. At a meeting of a dozen or so of us in 1967, he said he was willing, but only if each of us in the room would help. He insisted on what I think of as a loyalty oath. Everyone had to promise to participate actively and to take on some responsibility. For a time, I was the treasurer.

Although Lore shared my political inclinations, she showed no support for my activities. "Going out to save the world again?" was her repeated comment. She didn't like dinner and evening parties, and she was the first to want to leave. She cared little for my colleagues and even less for my graduate students. There was also her attitude toward sex, which she was ready to give up. I wasn't good at dealing with the conflicts and no doubt became more difficult to live with. The time came when I walked out without any confidence that we would get together again.

The uncertainty of not knowing where my life would lead was quite terrifying. I moved through the days in a fog and had little contact with Lore. After some time of living apart, she said she would consider a reconciliation, but only if we went to a marriage counselor. That led to another difficult time. During an early meeting, Pat, the counselor, asked us to describe something that we liked about each other. I went first and talked about Lore's reliability and straightforward ways, and how I admired her artistic abilities. When her turn came, she just sat there and couldn't think of anything. After a while I got up, said, "I don't need this," and left. Still, we continued to struggle, and after about six months we agreed to start living together again.

Our life was easier the second time around. We knew we didn't want to go back to the previous disruptive and contentious time. We had seen the limits of what we were willing to endure, and we were more solicitous of each other and more ready to compromise. I was ready to be more assertive. When Lore said that she would prefer separate beds, I didn't have to think about my answer: "I will never force you to sleep with me, but if you want separate beds I will no longer consider myself married to you."

At Pat's suggestion we opened separate bank accounts and put in a certain amount each year that was our own. I no longer had to make a case for every dollar that I wanted to spend. My salary was growing, and by that time my job was secure. That made a large difference because, until then, the uncertainties of my life were reflected and multiplied in Lore's fears and feelings of insecurity. The children were grown, or nearly so. Tommy was out of the house and Naomi was a teenager. With these sources of friction gone, there were fewer obstacles to a fresh beginning.

Lore still didn't like to see me going out to meetings, but we did quite a lot together. We went to museum exhibits and to all the shows and gallery openings of her wide circle of artist friends. As her work continued, it became more varied and no longer tied to the loom. She combined graphic elements with fiber constructions, and she had many exhibits of her own. In 1997 she had a retrospective at the Black Mountain Museum and Arts Center in Asheville, North Carolina, near where the college had been until it closed in 1956. It was accompanied by a comprehensive catalog and biography. In 2005 one of her pieces was featured next to that of her teacher, Anni Albers, in an exhibit called *High Fib*er at the Renwick Gallery in Washington, DC, which is part of the Smithsonian's American Art Museum.

Weavers often pay great attention to the use of natural and personally dyed and prepared fibers. Lore, however, liked to stress that she used the most modern materials, and delighted in telling surprised visitors that plastic raffia was one of her favorites. One of her works using this material is now on display in the Princeton Municipal Building.

Although Lore didn't like to spend money, she was sometimes ready to spend major amounts when she thought the expenditure would have a special impact on our lives. Vacations were in a favored category. When she talked about buying a vacation house, I objected, saying that we would never get to see any other place. We did buy a house in Vermont in 1974, soon after our reconciliation. It's a very small place that gave us great pleasure over the years and did not deter us from seeing quite a bit of the world after we bought it.

LORE: STROKE AND DEATH

Lore was healthy and was often called a role model. She continued to make fiber art until a week before she collapsed outside the house with a stroke, close to her 87th birthday.

The children got to the hospital as soon as they could, and when Naomi saw her in the emergency ward, unable to speak, attached to a variety of tubes, she said, "Do you think Mom would want to live this way?"

Both of us had living wills that asked that no heroic measures be taken to keep us alive when there was no hope of recovery to a sentient life, but it was not at all clear that this was the case now. I did not think that there was any alternative other than to wait. Not only that, but I thought I saw signs of vitality, a will to live, and small improvements. However, a few days later, Lore had a second episode and it became clear that she was severely affected.

She was in the hospital for some weeks and then was transferred to a rehabilitation unit. After a while she was able to eat, and I was there at mealtimes to feed her. She had physical therapy, and I again saw her astonishing determination to participate and to follow the instructions of the therapist. A physician of our acquaintance said that she would make progress for a couple of weeks, and then no more. He was wrong.

She continued to improve, but within severe limits. She had speech therapy, and learned to repeat simple phrases, but did not speak independently again. The nurses and aides were mostly kind, but the institutional atmosphere was stifling. I came to dread entering when I came to feed her in the morning and shutting the double doors behind me when I left in the evening. When she was moved to a depressing, supposedly permanent unit, I knew that I did not want to leave her there.

I had some changes made to our house, primarily in the bathroom, replacing the tub with a large, tiled shower area big enough for a chair, and adding support bars. We would also need a ramp at the entrance. I was fortunate to find a skilled and imaginative person in Doug Wales, who has since made many other improvements. Two people recommended a woman to stay in the house to help.

On the last day a therapist showed me how to maneuver Lore into the car, and I felt liberated when I took her home. The full-time helper was essential at the beginning when I knew nothing about what to do. But it didn't take long for her presence, her habits, and her person to become a major burden. When she refused to take Lore to the bathroom in the middle of the night because she said she couldn't fall asleep again, I impatiently said that I would do it, and I knew I had to make another change. Tina Santizo was recommended as a new caretaker, was very helpful, and became a friend. She came for a few hours four days a week, and I took care of the rest.

People are surprised when I say that this was a positive time for me. I knew Lore needed me, and there was an intimate closeness as I did what I had to do. I had Tina's help and learned to do everything, cooking for her, washing and cleaning her, giving her medicines and enemas, dressing her and going for walks with her in her wheelchair. We had two wheelchairs, one light traveling chair that we kept in the car, and one in the house and for walks in the neighborhood. I reveled in the attention and the priority that we got when we crossed the highway to go to a nearby park. I took her to friends, to exhibits, and to parties. If Lore recognized friends, she responded to them by raising her arm. It helped enormously to have the support of the children and of so many others. One day I left Doug with her while I went on an errand. She was able to indicate some essentials, and when I came back, he had put her on the toilet. Way beyond his normal duties. I thought how fastidious she had been, how concerned with her appearance and her privacy.

I don't know to what extent she was conscious of who I and others were, and I made no effort to find out. I kept thinking of the man who quit his job to take care of his mother who looked at him and said, "And who might you be?" I didn't want to let it get to that point. I was with her when she had an encephalogram. I held her hand, and I saw the flat line on one of the readouts. There was never a doctor's report, and no one ever said anything to me about the result, but there was nothing I needed to know. I read none of the books and articles that I was given. The only thing I learned is that every case is different and depends on the particular damage to the brain. What I saw was all there was for me.

She slept a good deal and when she did, I would go to my desk to work on the physics text that I had started. I wrote most of it during that time, and it was published soon afterward. I was determined not to become a hermit, and I paid helpers to stay with Lore when I wanted to go out. I turned down no invitations, and I went to more meetings than ever. The living room was improved with better lighting and a skylight. The improvements made it possible for me to host my recorder group, and to convene a political book discussion group that I chaired and other meetings. This was a major change, and a liberation.

Lore learned to propel her wheelchair and walk a little with a walker. She was just beginning to climb stairs when she started to slow down. It turned out to be a heart-valve defect. The sympathetic cardiologist said an operation was possible, but might very well be fatal, and did not encourage it. "If you're lucky, she'll die in her sleep." I looked at Lore, and I saw that I had no choice. I told the people who stayed with her when I was not there not to let her be taken to a hospital.

She became weaker, and one night I got into bed with her and held her as I often did. After a while I said good night, and she answered, "Good night." The next morning when Tina came early to give her a shower, she told me that Lore was not waking up. She had died peacefully in her sleep.

I called a friend and hospice social worker, Liz Cohen, and she stayed with me for some time. She said I needed to call the police and should take out the living will. Excellent advice. A few minutes later six men came running up to the house with a stretcher. I showed them the document and told them that I did not want them in the house. It was what I had been told so many times: at this difficult and vulnerable time it is easy to lose control, and for things to happen that you do not want.

As a ceremony, the cremation is for the survivors, and no longer for the dead. I arranged for the cheapest one and regretted it. After all, the container was just going to be there for the briefest time before it was burned, and I saw no point in spending money on it. I asked the Collcutts to come along, and it was for them and for me. When I saw the cardboard container, reminiscent of a mail-order package, I regretted my choice. I thought of Lore, and whether frugality would have won over her strong sense of esthetics.

The children and a few friends joined me when we scattered the ashes in a wooded area a short distance from the house. I read a poem by W. S. Merwin, and we planted a small tree.

The building of the Unitarian Congregation (no longer called a church) was beautiful and sufficiently non-denominational for a memorial meeting. Her work was displayed with a series of photomontages that Tommy had commissioned and designed, showing the aspects of her life. His friend Italo Gargione, who had a restaurant in Trenton, did the catering.

I wanted Lisa, as Lore's oldest friend, to be the first to speak. She was late and the people in the packed hall had to wait, but it all worked out. Other people spoke, and there were musical interludes with a group of my recorder-playing friends. Both children had warm and touching things to say, without glossing over some of the difficult aspects. I introduced the speakers and took the last part. After some words about Lore, I thanked the Unitarians for their hospitality, and said that I also wanted to pay homage to her Jewish heritage, and to say *Kaddish* for her.

It is sometimes called a prayer for the dead, but it is not a prayer, nor is there mention of the dead. It is an affirmation of God (where I prefer to use the term "spirit of the universe"). It is said before the congregation, to mark the continuity of the community. I said the lines, alternating the original Aramaic and English, as the end of the touching collective tribute.

INTERLUDE (2010)

Thursday was market day
rain in the morning
work in the afternoon
it was three
before I was out in the sun with my backpack
ready for the salad
the fruit
perhaps flowers
the smell
the feel
the abundance of the gifts of the earth

It wasn't there.
Had they gone home?
Was it the rain?
Or just the fear of rain?

I went on for my hour's walk
not thinking of other times

when I could see
the table set

on the other side of the door
and the door closing in my face
the fruit uneaten
the book unread
the kiss denied
suddenly a fantasy
created in my head
without the substance
of existence in the brightness of the day.

A flare lit up the sky for me

We live in the moment the next one
 is not
   the same
     the sun continues
we have learned to harvest even in the winter
when the fruit is paler
and flowers do not bloom
fondness
 perhaps love
   still there

When I woke up
in the middle of the night
for an instant
I thought you were there

II

rain
on the roof
all night

soothing accompaniment
to the thoughts
not all quiet

where are you
friend

new plants
waiting to be put in the ground
nurtured, fed
their thirst slaked
their leaves unbound

work
coming to a new stage
the labor of love
closer to the long-awaited birth
other hands must now help
will the world be kind to what is brought forth

soon the day
a gift renewed
ever fresh

III Song for X

today, tomorrow
and the next day

is it too much

what I see
with you

is more
than what I see
alone
alone
because
I see it with you

what I hear
with you
is more
than what I hear
alone
because I hear it
I hear it
with you

what I feel
with you
is more
than what I feel
alone
because I feel it
with you
with you

the hug you get
from me
is different
from all those
others
it comes with warmth
and love

you have that
and you need that
just as much
just as much

IV

you had called time out
but you were there
at the door
long coat
jet black
your face above it
and that luminous hair

you said you had something to bring
and I knew
that a gift
can be on the plus side
or not

a plate
thin slices
skin
then yellow
pink
blood red in the center
an open wound
guarded by a shell

it doesn't work for me you said
and left

I bit into a slice
it was bitter
harsh
bitter

I ate the rest
glad when it was gone.

Reprise: Bela, his cat, and Naomi

PART 7: REPRISE

PARENTS, REVISITED

In my childhood years in Vienna, I lived a rather isolated life. The women who took care of me did just that, they took care of my daily routine. Before I went to school, I saw more of them than of anyone else. They must have educated me in some minimal sense, but I have no memory of that, or of their presence or personalities. One is in some photographs, but she seems a stranger. And that's what she was. I was aware of her limited authority and of her impermanence.

My parents' work attenuated their role. My father's medical practice was in our apartment, so that he was always close by, but his was a largely passive presence. Years later, when I was asked what I could remember that my father contributed to my life and upbringing, I had to think hard. I finally remembered that he taught me to read before I started school. He made meticulous ornamented drawings of the letters with red and blue pencil on little squares of paper, and he used them to teach me to read.

I wonder how my memory distorts him. Was he really such a negative person? His nephew Herbert's wife Hanna remembered him that way. She spoke about a visit to him, and her relief when they finally left, as a dark cloud lifting. My feelings were also affected by my mother's attitude and the alienation between them. As I look back, it seems to me that he didn't really take me seriously. He and a friend regularly got together to play chess. He showed me the moves but made little attempt to go further. He said he couldn't play with such a *Patzer*, someone who knew so little.

He may have tried. One time he started a conversation by saying, "Was denkst du dir… (What comes to your mind) when you read, 'He loves her, she loves him?'" I tensed up, thinking, "Here it is." I knew what was coming and I didn't know how to cope with it. I put on my best stupid face and answered "*gar nichts*" ("I don't think of anything"). That was the end of my sex education. He gave up.

Medical achievements in Vienna were legendary. Kings and princes came to Vienna with their ailments because of this reputation. My father was very conscious of being a product of his schooling in this environment, but I learned little from him about the work that he did. This was the time between the two world wars. Medical practice was far from what we see today. I have already mentioned the ultraviolet irradiations and the enigmatic arsenic tonic that he subjected me to. Years later I showed him a skin problem on my arm, mostly to encourage him to revive his interest and to use his expertise. He took an ancient volume from his shelf and said, "We used to give mercury for that." This time I was able to flee. As I also did when he suggested irrigations for a prostate problem.

He had his own formulations for the ointments that he prescribed and found a pharmacist in Vancouver who was willing to make up the mixtures for his patients in accord with his detailed instructions. This was not only unheard of, but it was against the rules that left the choice of a pharmacy up to the client. He was charged by the medical organization and told to stop telling his patients which pharmacy to choose. I'm not sure what happened, but he may have mixed his own after that.

My mother suffered from back pains. She was variously treated with leeches and cobra poison. She pleaded for pain-killers. My father refused to give her the opioids that she wanted, which may have been the right thing to do. In any case, it did not ease the tense atmosphere. It's an illustration of the way he was: stern and firm with others, although he could be whiny and squeamish about himself.

He spent an hour in the bathtub every morning. That was just one of the things that led my mother to say, "He will live forever, because he takes such good care of himself." Personal hygiene was very important to him, and that served him well during his imprisonment in the Buchenwald concentration camp and his internments in England and Australia.

He was on the six-week voyage to Australia on the ship *Dunera*, which became infamous for the abusive treatment of its prisoners. One of the few things my father told me about it was that some were even robbed of their last possessions. The voyage was brought up as a scandal in the British parliament. The "passengers" elected my father minister of sanitation, and he held them to a strict regime of cleanliness. He may have made them even more miserable than they already were, but he may also have saved them from illness and death. I regret that I was not more insistent in questioning him. By being sensitive about his feelings, I learned nothing about his time on the ship or in the camps.

Years later I saw a notice of the film *The Boys of the Dunera*,, and I rushed to see it. It was nothing like what I expected. As a result of my father's reticence, I had no frame of reference, but the group of religious Jews it portrayed had no counterpart in my imagination. I guess I expected them to be more like the assimilated intellectuals of my acquaintance.

* * * * *

In 1942, my father was finally released from the Australian internment camp, and I went to meet him when his boat docked in Vancouver. It was the year after I finished high school, when I had the various office-boy jobs. We lived side-by-side in a small room. He studied English by reading the dictionary, starting with "A." He wanted to speak English with me, but that was tedious, and we fell back to speaking German to each other. He insisted that it be unadulterated: speak English or German, but don't mix them up! *Keine Mischkulanz!* I owe it to this insistence that my German has remained good.

He got the certificate that allowed him to take the exam for his medical license without delay and without the obstacles that were put in my mother's way, and he set about assiduously studying the heavy textbooks. He was now 60 years old. When he eventually succeeded, he opened a modest dermatological practice, but he did not attempt to become a certified specialist.

He never learned to drive. During the time when I lived at home, I taught my mother to drive, and he watched as she was backing up in our driveway, going erratically back and forth. "That woman will never drive," was his comment, which summed up a good deal of the kind of response and support that could be expected from him, as well as his attitude toward her. When I left for New York and graduate school, he said, "When will all this school come to an end?" He may have thought that his own security was at risk as long as I didn't have a job, ready to help him.

Let me not get this wrong: he was my father. I did not admire him, but I felt close to him, with feelings of love, and I did what I could to take care of him. He came to visit us in Princeton about every two years and we paid for his tickets and all expenses. His main contribution was to cook for us once or twice, usually *Wiener Schnitzel* (breaded veal cutlets) or *Palatschinken* (Viennese pancakes). At the table he would often start by saying that something had gone wrong. In fact, it was always good, and he got the expected praise. After he was done, there was a major mess in the kitchen, with every pan used and batter on every surface, including the floor and the ceiling.

It was tough to take him out to a restaurant, because he kept comparing the cost and quality to what he could do at home. What did not happen, and what has left an unresolved conflict for me, is that we did not invite him to move in with us. He openly lobbied for that, but it was at a time when the relationship between Lore and me was strained, and we could barely cope with each other. My father loved Lore, and she could do no wrong in his eyes. Once, during a visit when our hostility came out into the open, he came close to crying and wanted to go home immediately. The crisis passed, but the stain on the relationships remained.

He spent the last month of his life in a continuing care facility. Just before he moved there, I spent several weeks with him in his house. I didn't know whether my marriage with Lore would survive and was ready to spend some time away from it. The relationship with my father was close and intimate, but again I learned almost nothing about his early life or his family. I took care of his food, would buy some wine, and the traditional *Le Chaim* ("To life!") took on special meaning. When I remarked on all the butter and eggs that he had for breakfast, he said, "You know, it really doesn't matter!" and I saw the foolishness of my concern.

I was home again when I got the call that he was near the end. I could find a night flight only as far as Seattle, and in that last frantic scramble to Vancouver I almost ran out of gas in the rental car. I was soon holding his hand as I sat on his bed at the facility where he lived. He refused the bedpan when he needed to urinate, and he stood up one more time while I held him. He tried to tell me something but couldn't talk anymore. He tried to write it on a piece of paper, but could only move the pen back and forth. I was apprehensive, terrified that he would exhort me to reconcile with Lore, but I couldn't bring myself to say anything about that. I was far from certain what would happen and not optimistic. I could not tell what his own last thoughts were, and they may have been quite different. His last breath came soon, and after he was taken from the room, I went to his house to sleep. I had been sitting with him on the edge of the bed in a twisted, uncomfortable position, and the next morning my back was so paralyzed that I couldn't walk and could barely move. I dragged myself to the outside steps of the house with the telephone and made the calls to tell family and friends of his death.

My father had been with me at my mother's cremation five years earlier, and I had asked him about his wishes. He said, "I was born a Jew, and I want to die as a Jew." Now the time had come. He had never attended religious services on his own. One of his colleagues had seen this and paid for his attendance at his synagogue during the "high" holidays in the week between Rosh Hashanah and Yom Kippur.

There was a small gathering with some of his friends and acquaintances, presided over by a Cantor Nixon. He asked me to choose some attendees to be pallbearers. One was a neighbor who had become a friend and had been helpful to my father during the years that he lived alone in the small house that he bought after he and my mother separated. Cantor Nixon had one look at him and asked whether he was Jewish. Told that he was not, he asked me to find someone else. I was appalled and outraged. I wanted to walk out. I stood there seething, and I had to ask myself to what extent I was prepared to disrupt my father's last gathering. What would he have done? I asked an acquaintance who shared my father's refugee background to step in.

Cantor Nixon was not at the cemetery, and the person who was in charge there asked our friend who had been dismissed as pallbearer to step forward to a place of honor. There was a brief ceremony, the casket was lowered into the grave, and I was the first to throw a shovelful of earth.

* * * * *

My mother was a very different person, and she had a vastly larger impact on my life. She was responsible for sending me to the progressive elementary school that I attended for three years after my first year in the public school, just as she was always looking for more lessons, courses, friends, and experiences for me. She wanted to know each day what I had been doing, and when I had questions, or needed help, or was in trouble, she was the one that I turned to. She provided the initiative and energy to get herself and me, and later my father, out of Vienna, and she shaped the life that we had after that. She was adventurous and imaginative, always the dominant and the more active person in the family.

While I lived with my parents, I invariably took my mother's side in the disputes between them, and it took me a long time to acknowledge to myself that she was not always right, and that she, too, had flaws. She was 28 when I was born. I doubt that she interrupted her work for long. Once, after her death, my father told me that she had a number of abortions before my birth, and that he "had trouble preserving me." Her preoccupation with me was so great that my way of dealing with this story was, and continues to be, simply not to believe it, and to ascribe it to vindictiveness and passive revenge on his part.

I know next to nothing about their life before I was born. My father, fifteen years older, graduated in 1910 and served in the First World War in the Austro-Hungarian army, where he became *Oberarzt* (principal physician). He prided himself on his masculinity and once said, "I was never without a girl."

I doubt that there was a parallel to that in my mother's life. I only knew her with a strong wall of protective privacy about herself. In contrast to the modest apartment in an outlying district of Vienna where we had our home and my father's office, my mother's place of work in my grandmother's apartment in the Rotenturmstrasse couldn't have been more central. The plaque on the door read Dr. Elda Lindenfeld-Lachs, *Kosmetik*, using both her married and maiden names.

A large number of the women who became her patients did so because they were dissatisfied with the way they looked, and her experience with their poor self-image led to her interest in psychiatry and her association with Alfred Adler. Once she had her medical license in Vancouver, she called herself a psychiatrist, and that's what she then was. She was "board certified" as soon as that was available to her, and after a medical school was established at the University of British Columbia, she became a member of the teaching faculty as a clinical instructor, participating in conferences about patients and taking students on hospital rounds.

Nevertheless, she felt herself an outsider. Her relationship to the medical establishment, and particularly with her psychiatric colleagues, remained difficult, largely because they were hostile to Freudian psychoanalysis and to all the forms, such as Adler's, that developed from it. On the other hand, she got solid and continuing support from the social-work community. She had a devoted following there and saw it as an effective outlet for her energy and her ideas. She designed and taught a course on family dynamics at the UBC School of Social Work and had weekly meetings with groups from the Children's Aid Society and other agencies, where she discussed and gave advice on cases that were presented to her.

At some point, my mother, whom I called Elda by then, read *Science and Sanity* by Alfred Korzybski, and it made quite an impression on her. I read some of the large volume also and the tenet that I remember best concerns the different "levels of abstraction." As soon as you talk about something, write about it or make a picture, what you have is no longer the "thing" itself. The picture and the words are abstractions that describe it only in part. "The word is not the thing." Nor are other symbols. Obama was vilified for not wearing a flag pin, but the pin is not patriotism. The way a person looks, and his or her background, are not the person. It may seem obvious, but the violations of this principle confront us every day. As you can see, I was influenced also.

Elda found out that a fellowship was available for a stay at Korzybski's Institute for General Semantics in Chicago. She had never been to the United States, applied, and was accepted. Her week at the Institute was a chapter in her search for new ideas.

Korzybski made "General Semantics" more than wordplay: the central idea that words and symbols are just that, abstractions, and not "the thing," stayed with Elda, and stays with me. It made me more aware and careful about the use of language. Korzybski put a design that he called the "structural differential" on the wall. The exercise was to point at it while putting your hand over your mouth, as a reminder that as soon as you say something, you are using words, abstractions, and not the thing itself.

When Elda reached the age of 65, she got a curt letter saying that her university appointment was now ended. She showed it to me and said "*Jetzt bin ich beim alten Eisen*" (literally, "Now I'm with the scrap iron"). She was close to tears, partly because of the cold and impersonal manner of the termination, but mainly because her place at the university had meant a great deal to her as proof that she had "made it" in a professional environment that so often rejected her and what she stood for. I knew something about the determination that it had taken her to get to this point. She often referred to one or the other of two sayings that symbolized for me an essential ingredient of her nature and personality. The first was from an old copy of *Reader's Digest*. "On the plains of hesitation lie the bones of countless millions, who, at the dawn of victory, sat down to rest, and resting, died." The other one came from the world of baseball, a game about which she knew nothing, from a book containing the story "Don't Die on Third. Its title became her second mantra. It was about a player who got to third base near the end of a game, with just one out remaining. There was a detailed explanation of what it would take to steal home, and then the description of what went on in the player's mind until he did, in fact, score.

I seem to have inherited some of that persistence. There were times when her model of grittiness kept me going until I came to the end of a task. Sometimes I stayed with the path I was on even when it was not obvious that it was the wisest choice, or when it was not clear where it would lead or how far I would get. That's what happened when my job at Rutgers seemed to have come to an end, and I kept going without looking for another until I had rescued it. When I was discouraged and uncertain how to continue with tasks and assignments, she would say, "Don't die on third!" She understood that to reach third base gets you close to your goal, but that unless you take that essential last step, you are left with nothing.

She had the generous, giving nature that I associated with

the Mediterranean sun of her birthplace. She did not see that expansiveness in my father, or later in Lore. She criticized me sharply when she thought that I was being narrow or self-centered. When my father lived alone after my parents separated, we supported him to some extent. His sister Irma, my cousin Herbert's mother, had fled to Brazil, and my father told us that he sent her money from time to time. We did not see the necessity for him to give away some of "our" contribution, and we told him so. When my mother heard about this she was outraged. "During the war, in England, at the hostel for refugee children, we made sure that even when they had almost nothing, they got a little extra so that they would be able to give something to others."

Lore, on the other hand, did not like to spend or give away money. "When you really need it, you never have enough," she said. She often talked about Elda's profligate spending habits and how she dreaded having to take care of her one day. In the end, it was Lore who needed to be taken care of, and I was happy that I had the resources to do it.

Soon after I left for graduate school in New York, my parents separated. This had been coming for a long time, and the friction between them had become unbearable to Elda. I saw many ways that she felt stifled by my father, feeling unable to live her own life. He was in charge of the outside of the house and would present her with bills without letting her have a say. He cooked, and it was always the kind of heavy meals that she tried to avoid. She began to prepare her own food, while still cleaning all the encrusted frying pans that he used. She was embarrassed by him when they were invited out. He would sit in a corner saying nothing, until he heard his *Stichwort* (cue), when he would launch into one of his standard stories, such as the one about the classmates who brought him the money that allowed him to continue in school. The stories were often long and convoluted, and everyone was forced to listen to them while my mother cringed. Some people made a point of saying how they loved his stories, but my mother was not one of them. Their lives had become more and more separate, and I don't know of any attempts to overcome the divide. In her professional life my mother was able to help many to deal with difficult situations, but here, for herself and for him, she could not do what she did for her patients. I don't know to what extent it was my father's narrowness or whether her usual generosity and understanding for other people were just not there for him.

Some of the same feelings arose in her relationship with her sister. When we left Vienna, Alice (the Tante Litschi of my childhood) and her family did also, but only went as far as Brussels, the capital of Belgium, except for my cousin Renate, who managed to get to England. Belgium was soon occupied by the Nazi forces, and after the war started, the family was hidden. One day Erika walked out impatiently and did not come back. The records show that she died in the extermination chambers of Bergen-Belsen when she was 23. Renate, in England, was studying to be a nurse when she died in an air raid, also 23 years old. Willi stepped off a streetcar, slipped, and was run over. Elda and Alice's mother, my grandmother, had been living in Trieste. Near the end of the war, she was deported to Germany and died in the death camp of Auschwitz. She was 71. Alice was alone.

After the war my mother tried to help her sister to join her in Canada, but after a time she gave up. Alice knew no English, and it wasn't clear what she would do. She lived in a small apartment in Brussels, and it wasn't obvious where she would be better off. My suspicion is also that Elda was not ready to take on the burden of living with her sister. Alice had little education and represented a past that Elda had worked hard to free herself from, a past when women lived severely constricted lives. I don't think she was ready to give up the freedom she had achieved.

Once when I was in Europe for a conference, I stayed with Alice for a few days. She was very appreciative and showed me around a little. Later, while my family and I were in France on a sabbatical, we visited her. Each time, when it came time to go, she said, "*Was, du gehst schon?*" (You're leaving already?) But she would have said that no matter how long we'd been there. It was hard to be confronted with what she had lost and what she now had left.

Elda's experience of losing everything when she left Vienna led her to say that she would never again become attached to "things" and possessions. She didn't stick to that resolve. She was too intent on showing that she had overcome all obstacles and that she had "arrived." She bought a car that was too expensive, had clothes and hats made to order, acquired jewelry, furniture, native art, and, after she separated from my father, a house in Vancouver's best neighborhood. She went on trips and spent whatever money she had. When she died, the house was all she had.

Her relationship with Lore quickly deteriorated and continued to get worse. Lore saw her as someone who wanted to hang on to me and interfere with us, and she feared that Elda's improvidence would eventually cause her to depend on us. Elda saw Lore as someone who would not take her advice or follow her expectations. When we visited her in Vancouver shortly after we got married, she wanted to give a large party for us. Lore insisted that she was uncomfortable in large groups and, to my mother's disappointment, did what she could to resist. She was harsh and dismissive, and there was no party. I did not know how to intervene.

Whenever Elda called on the telephone, Lore would wave

to me after a short time to indicate that the call had gone on long enough. Elda came about once a year to visit us. She would announce when she would arrive, come without asking us about our schedule and how that time would work for us. When she got to New York, she would spend the day there, perhaps buying a new hat, and Lore resented that this should be a higher priority than coming to us. On observing Tommy with other people, she once commented, "He always goes to the men in the room," implying an approval of the way I handled my role as a father and an attack on Lore.

As I look back on these situations, I wish I had handled them better. Today, with more self-confidence, I think I could do that. Then, however, I saw myself caught between the two. I felt that it was my place to support Lore, but I was unhappy that it meant rejecting my mother.

Elda, of course, wanted more phone calls, more letters, more attention, and more participation in our lives. Lore was working and also trying to take care of the children as best she could. She found Elda's visits stressful and eventually said that she just didn't have the necessary energy. She asked me to tell Elda that she would have to stay at a hotel. That's what happened, but Elda made it clear that she would never forgive Lore or me. It was her last visit.

At about that time, a year or two before Elda's death, I received a letter from the head of the physics department at UBC, suggesting that I apply for a position to replace a departing faculty member whose specialty overlapped mine. When Lore heard about it, she said that she would never want to live in the same city as my mother. It wasn't going to happen anyway, because it was clear to me that UBC wanted a person with a greater commitment to research than I was ready for. I declined, saying that I was too involved in my projects at Rutgers. I said nothing about the job offer to Elda, but shortly after I refused the invitation, she was at a party also attended by the department head who had written me. He went over to her and said, "Your son could at least have come to visit and talked with us." She was devastated, and I cannot avoid thinking that the disappointment contributed to her death.

She lived at a far different pace than my father. She took everything more seriously, and looked at everything more emotionally, more passionately, including her work, her friends, and me. She did not take care of herself. When she needed to sleep, she took sleeping pills. When she needed to be up, she took stimulants. When I found this out and objected, she simply said, "This is what I have to do." She knew she had heart problems, but I doubt that she received or followed proper care.

The phone call came one evening: She had died of a heart attack while she was with a patient. She was 70 years old. Her body was taken to a Jewish cemetery, but I knew she would not want that and asked that it be taken to a secular funeral home. When I arrived, I asked to see her. There is no "cult of the body" among Jews, nor was there for her, but I sat in the room alone with her and my thoughts before getting up to face what I needed to do. I made arrangements for a memorial meeting for some weeks later.

* * * * *

When I came home Lore and I embraced, and I said, "Now there is nothing to stand between us." That's not how it worked out. She resented the time I spent answering people who wrote about my mother and then writing to many more. I was disappointed that she couldn't let me mourn in my way.

Here is what I read in the filled hall at the memorial.

December 13, 1967

Dear Tommy and Naomi,

This letter is for you because you are her grandchildren.

You know Elda as a grandmother whom you saw only for a few days at a time. I want you to know a little more about her, about the kind of person she was, and about the kind of life that she lived.

I am flying over Canada, passing over the country that I first crossed with her, nearly 30 years ago. I was about as old as you are now, Tommy, but I was a thin, tuberculous child. I was all she had—my father was in a concentration camp in Germany that few survived—and she fought like an animal protecting her young to get me and herself away from the horror that was descending on the Jews in Europe. We were in a train from Montreal to Vancouver for four days—I still remember the black seats and the stuffiness of the air. Another boy gave me some comic books. I had never seen anything like them and didn't understand them. We were in a country that had only been a page in a geography book for us, where people spoke a language that Elda knew only slightly, and I not at all.

She had to start a completely new life. There were many people who helped, but it was her courage, her drive and determination that I want to tell you about today.

Her eyes had always been bad, but now she worked for years, squinting and straining, removing hair from women's faces. She hated the work, but it was a start, and in the meantime, I could go to school. After many years, when she had become successful, she loved to buy things, and to have things, perhaps to remind herself that those hard, early years had really passed.

But before that she herself had to go to school again. At a time when others enter the most productive years of their career, she was still struggling to become established. I think her year at the University of Manitoba was a happy one. She had to borrow money to go, but she was more carefree than I remember her at any other time, enjoying her life as a student, surrounded by young people and friends. When she came back to Vancouver, life was quite different. My father had come, I was going to university, and she started her medical practice. She believed that what the world needed most was more sanity. She worked all her life to bring people closer to sanity, to an understanding of themselves and an understanding of others. She believed that on the largest scale, peace between people and between peoples would come when more individuals had this understanding, this sanity, themselves. She brought her whole warmth and humanity to her work, and it was here that she came closest to fulfilment. She helped many people and she was loved and admired by many people for what she did. It is a rare kind of person who has the wisdom and insight that this work requires. She had this gift to a very high degree. Sometimes it failed her, sometimes she was not able to use it with herself or some of those closest to her.

I think with shame and sadness of the times when I caused her sorrow, and of the opportunities for giving her pleasure that I did not use. I am happy as I think of the love that she had for me and for you and of the meaning that my life and your lives gave to hers.

December 14, 1967

I had to stop writing. We were approaching Vancouver. It was one of those luminous days when every wave on the ocean, every tree on the mountains, stood out clearly as I looked down on the scene that she loved so much.

Yesterday I went to see her—but I didn't see her. I see

her now, with her full vitality, surrounded by her friends, touching them with her capacity for love, for enjoyment, for emotion.

She died the way she wanted to die. She was at her desk, with a patient, and it was over right away. She was in the midst of work, of buying presents, of making plans.

I am grateful that she was spared a period of inactivity, of failing, of invalidism. I am grateful that we still had a time together a few weeks ago.

Elda only rarely came close to inner peace and serenity. She always wanted more—more physical activity, more mental activity—to see more, to do more, help more, and give more and understand more. She might have been happier had she been able to be more passively accepting, but that was not her way.

I believe, as she believed, that our lives have meaning only through our contact with others. I believe, as she believed, that there is only one kind of life after death—that which continues in other people. People whose life you have touched, perhaps enriched, sometimes gladdened, sometimes saddened. Elda loved people and she will continue to live in the hearts and minds of many.

You are links in the chain of which she was a part. I see in you her inner and outer beauty, her restlessness, her generosity, her appeal to people, and her love for people. She will continue to live in you as in your life you continue hers. She will continue to live in you as in your lives you continue toward the fulfilment of her dreams.

RETURN TO VANCOUVER, 1996

There are days when the air is so clear and transparent that we feel we can see farther than we ever have before. The distant is suddenly close, the haze is gone. Sometimes that feeling turns inward. We see ourselves as never before, as the clarity illuminates dark corners that we have kept hidden.

This was such a day. I was in Vancouver for the first time in years on a journey to the past. I spent the day visiting the neighborhoods where I had lived for a decade. Each stone was familiar to me as I went from place to place, the vividness of my memory renewed by the reality before me.

I was fourteen when my mother arrived here with me, fleeing the darkness that had descended over Europe. Her marriage and her career were suspended. The environment was alien, sometimes hostile. Slowly, painfully, it became home. My father joined us later, but it was she who had taken the initiative and was responsible for our survival, for our being here.

It was late afternoon as I drove toward the ocean. I rounded a corner and saw the sun, large and red, close to the horizon. I began to race to get to the point on the beach where I wanted to see it go down. I passed up several places where I might have had a good view, and realized, going downhill on the last stretch, that I would be too late. I parked the car and climbed down the embankment. The sun was gone.

I looked over the quiet sea, first to the right, to the city buildings across the bay, then straight across, to the mountains. The first layer rises almost from the water. Then come the layers beyond, the peaks, the ranges, finally the glaciers, still glistening in the glow of the evening. The colors change, dark green to bluish gray, each one against the background of the farther layer, and eventually against the sky. Each line was sharp, the blue, even in the distance, more intense than I had seen it before.

The last time I was here I had scattered my mother's ashes at the water's edge. I had no doubt then that she would have approved. She loved the city and the ocean and the mountains, and she often came to this spot to swim. Yet I might not have chosen this area if I had known that it would become a nude beach.

Her attitude toward nudity was mixed. There was the streak of defiant freethinking, abstract and intellectual, and also the fearful protection of her private self, hurt too often, unwilling to risk exposure. She always encouraged me to be bolder than she thought she had been and hoped that I would go beyond the bounds that seemed to hold her back.

Was she disappointed in me? One day she looked at my son and said, "He always reminds me of you. But he is so much freer." Perhaps it is easier today to escape some outer constraints. But who among us is free of the shackles within?

The beach was almost deserted. Some distance away a group was preparing a fire for a picnic. I took off my clothes and walked into the water. I swam toward the mountains, still clear and close. The water was smooth, shimmering, reflecting, distorting, as mountains and reflections merged. I closed my eyes to feel the intimate motion against me.

I like to swim long distances. Once, years ago, I had swum across the bay. How far would I get today? What were the chances that molecules from my mother's body were around me now? I felt her presence as part of the clarity of the vision before me, now darkening, but still bold and near. I wanted to go on until I, too, would merge, more closely yet, to become part of the sea that contained her. Was it from the inside or the outside that I felt the pull to go on?

Reality was no longer important as I floated, my eyes now half closed, aware only of the water moving along me. Was it time for the haze to come back, for the outlines of the mountains to disappear into the homogeneity of night?

I shook myself free and turned back.

When I got close to the beach, I saw that it was full of people. No one was nude. Couples were sitting on the rocks, groups were roasting hot dogs. They seemed self-absorbed enough, but as the only person in the water, I felt wildly conspicuous. My earlier mood of mystical union gave way to panic as I tried to decide which way to turn. There seemed no way except to face the exposure that I knew only from nightmares.

I dressed myself in nonchalance and exhibitionism and strode out. A couple was sitting next to my clothes. The boy had a camera poised. They looked at me briefly, and I was grateful for their lack of interest. Moments later I was scrambling up the hill.

THE NEW GENERATION UNFOLDS

In America, even those who do not follow the usual and generally accepted path can sometimes flourish. One can go through life in steps that do not follow a set, predictable pattern, in spite of the pervasive, and usually inflexible, bureaucracies. The system is often chaotic. It works well for some, but it can also work badly, especially for those with no help or role model who flounder as they try to navigate it.

Tommy's progress was a source of special joy to me. I had been active in the local Democratic organization, and I viewed him as my gift to the Democratic Party. I participated vicariously in his political life, and I saw myself wistfully in him. His progress was extraordinary. I had complete confidence in him and thought he could change the world. In fact, he came pretty close to doing it.

After Tommy's graduation he worked on various New Jersey Democratic political staff jobs and campaigns. In 1988, he was the campaign manager for Frank Pallone, the candidate for Congress in a New Jersey district that had been held by Republicans. *Campaigns and Elections Magazine* called it "the best-run House campaign in the country." Pallone won (he is still a leading progressive Democrat in the House of Representatives), and Tommy became his chief of staff. Tom later had various other jobs in Washington, including Director of Elections for the Democratic National Committee.

He became a partner of David Axelrod (who was later an advisor to President Obama) and then founded his own company, which became a prominent consulting firm in DC. I remember his work on the 2006 gubernatorial and congressional campaigns in Pennsylvania, where he organized a whole fleet of vans to serve as transportation and mobile offices for staff and volunteers. He was constantly on the go, checking, supervising, and handling problems. As a result of these and other efforts, four districts changed from being Republican to representation by Democrats. He made a difference. For Obama's 2004 Senate campaign, he managed the get-out-the-vote effort in some of Chicago's African-American areas. After Obama was elected to the Senate, he gave Tommy a copy of his book *Dreams from my Father*, and inscribed it, "Thanks for helping to get me here." In early 2007, Tommy went on to organize some of the largest rallies of the Obama presidential campaign.

How about Naomi? Is she getting overshadowed again by her louder brother? She found her own way to develop her skills and pursue her dreams. When she graduated from Princeton High School, she knew she wanted to go to college, but without the usual stressful and competitive academic atmosphere. She chose the *Program in Artisanry* at Boston University where she could concentrate on ceramics. She graduated in 1980 with an education that gave her the basis to become the professional potter she is today. She went on to work with several potters in the classic progression from apprentice to journeyman to master.

In 1983, Naomi and some fellow potters founded the cooperative Brattleboro Clayworks in Brattleboro, Vermont. By that time, she had settled on a Japanese technique that she has pursued and developed ever since. Clay is dyed and rolled into layers, then carved to bring different layers to the surface producing intricate designs. She primarily makes objects for household use and sells them in shops and at craft fairs but has also explored sculptural work. They have been described in books and shown in exhibits. In addition, Naomi teaches in the art department of the Putney School, a residential high school in Putney, Vermont. In 2005, an exhibit at the Brattleboro Museum called "Lindenfeld-Lindenfeld Dialogue" displayed pieces by mother and daughter side-by-side, showing how Naomi used Lore's textiles as inspiration for her own work.

Naomi met her husband Michael at a contradance when she was 42. She joined him in the UMass outing club, a group of people initially at the University of Massachusetts who go on hikes and rafting trips together, some of whom have remained close friends. They had a beautiful wedding on an apple farm near their Brattleboro home. One of their friends, a justice of the peace, officiated. There was a lot of singing and dancing, and even a little recorder music in which I collaborated with a guitar-playing friend of theirs. The day ended with a procession up a hill at twilight. The following morning the celebration continued with breakfast and strawberry picking.

The farm was next door to a house that Naomi rented for us, called Naulakha, built by Rudyard Kipling when he lived in Vermont for some years. A small plaque said that this is where he wrote *The Jungle Book*. It was a special treat for Lisa, Lore, and our families to live in Kipling's house for a few days.

Both Naomi and Michael are active in their community. Michael is on energy- and conservation-oriented bodies and committees, Naomi in arts organizations. Her studio is in their basement, with a kiln next to it. The outing club is still part of the family, with hiking and occasional excursions into the wilderness.

Over the years Naomi has participated in African dance classes and has helped organize them and bring teachers to this country from Africa. That led to an invitation from a dance teacher to come to Senegal. She and Michael stayed in the house of the teacher's family. Naomi got dance lessons, and both enjoyed their immersion in Senegal's culture.

My own look at some of what they experienced came during a visit to Brattleboro when Naomi took me to one of the dance evenings. About 20 people were there, some in colorful clothes, with the African teacher and three African drummers. It took only a short warm-up for the group to reach an almost frenzied state of high energy, with a steady rhythm and an all-enveloping intensity. The whole building shook and it was hard to sit still.

When Naomi was a child, she was so quiet that we sometimes worried how she would fare in an often-unforgiving world. It took her some time, but she became confident and sure of herself and her work, "centered" in the sense that the word has been applied both to work on the potter's wheel and to personal development by M. C. Richards. MC, as she was called, was a faculty member at Black Mountain College, where she became a friend of Lore's. She later wrote *Centering in Pottery, Poetry and the Person* (Wesleyan University Press, 1964), which became something of a cult classic among young women. The photograph that I took of MC and Naomi looking together at a display of MC's work hangs in Naomi's studio.[11]

AT THE EDGE OF THE FUTURE

Shall I go on with anecdotes and memories? So much comes back as I think of what I have not said.

Mary Clurman and I are an unlikely couple. We met when she gave a presentation at an environmental film festival about her time volunteering on organic farms in France and Britain, and I asked a friend who seemed to know her to introduce us. She tells me that we had met earlier in the hospital after Lore's stroke, when Mary was there as well, recovering from a serious accident. She had volunteered for the Peace Corps in her 60s and was working in Thailand when a dog ran out in front of her bicycle and caused her to fall. She received some care; but when her injuries led to an abdominal infection, she was flown to Princeton and her brother Joe's house, where she was living when we met at the film festival.

Her earlier experiences were different from mine, and perhaps more debilitating, with two less-than-fulfilling marriages. Her son Will has become a friend. I think of him and his two children as members of my family and the best outcome of her earlier life.

Mary and I were both quite ready for affection and warmth. We explore the world together, both near and far. We learn from each other, make adjustments as we encounter conflicts, care for each other, and enjoy our emotional and physical closeness.

The outdoors is Mary's domain. When we began living together in 2011, she said she would like to plant vegetables in front of the house, the only place where there is some sun. I saw that as an intrusive change in my environment and objected. It took me some time to get used to this and other transformations. When vegetables began to appear, I became an enthusiastic consumer.

* * * * *

I hear Mary practicing her chorus role in Brahms' *German Requiem* with its bass solo, "*Herr, lehre doch mich, dass ein Ende mit mir haben muss, und mein Leben ein Ziel hat, und ich davon muss, und ich davon muss, davon muss.*" ("Teach me that my life will have an end, and a purpose, and that I must leave, that I must leave, must leave.") It's a great and solemn musical line that I like to listen to without thinking about religion or death. Still, I know the sequence, as we all do.

* * * * *

The children's religious education was haphazard. When Tommy started first grade, we enrolled him in a Jewish Sunday school.

That lasted only one semester, because we had difficulty accepting the mix of Bible stories and chauvinistic history. At the same time, we valued shared thoughts and celebrations, and often built them around Jewish holidays. When Tommy was close to his 13th birthday, we talked with him about a Bar Mitzvah, the traditional occasion when a boy is accepted into the community and called up at a Sabbath service to read a passage from the Torah.

There was no question of his reading in Hebrew, but he agreed to do it at home, in English. The selection was left to me, but it was not easy to find a passage with universal, understandable meaning. We settled on the very beginning, the creation of the world. Tommy asked a few friends to come, and there were neighbors, including Lee Dratfield, who sang some Jewish songs, and Lore's parents. Naomi and I played a recorder duet, I said a few words, and Lore's father gave a blessing. Our living room was transformed by the festive occasion.

There were other traditional celebrations. We invited friends for Chanukah meals, and made a special effort for Passover, generally including some non-Jewish guests. This is the holiday that celebrates the liberation of the Jews from slavery in Egypt. The youngest child asks what the day is about, triggering a recitation of the history, accompanied by ceremonial drinking, eating, singing, and a good deal of talk.

My memories of the family gatherings in Vienna were still vivid and helped us to sustain the tradition. The core is the reading of the Haggadah, the book that outlines the history and. the sequence of the evening. It exhorts us to keep the traditions alive and to renew them. One year I took this command seriously and wrote a Haggadah with illustrations taken from various versions, which my children have used. One feature that has encouraged them is that it is shorter than the traditional one. For me it was more important to use modern language, and to confront the crueler passages, such as those about the plagues that were visited on the Egyptians.

* * * * *

A related experience that I think of fondly is from the day when I received the Millikan award. A group of teachers from New Jersey surrounded me on the steps, and one of them said a Hebrew blessing: *Baruch atah Adonai, Elohenu Melech haolam, shehechianu, vekimanu, vehigianu lazman haseh*. Blessed are You, Lord, our God, king of the universe, who has granted us life, and lifted us up, and allowed us to reach this time.

Here is my free adaptation; "Blessed are you, spirit of the universe, that has given us life, sustained us, and has allowed us to see this day."

* * * * *

Is our existence miraculous? A miracle is something that we don't understand. But the expectation can remain that with study and greater knowledge we can get closer to an understanding. I feel close to the way Albert Einstein thought when he referred to the rules made by *Der Alte*, "the old one."

* * * * *

The language we use tells us so much about our feelings. Mary's language is often different from mine. In the morning she likes to quote the verse she first heard from her mother, "This is the day that the Lord has made. Let us be glad and rejoice in it." It starts the day on a wonderful optimistic note. It also implies that the time is not only our own. It is "made," miraculously, magically.

We live in "ordinary" time, as it unrolls, one moment after the other, never repeating, always new. That's the way Newton saw it in the 16th century, and most of the time we do too. But "magical" time is never far from us. We use it as we celebrate holidays, as we live in our imagination, as we struggle with the limitations of our understanding.

My parents battled the "medieval" and ancient thinking that is dominated by unknown forces and beings which has held people back and away from the quest for greater understanding. It is a struggle for most of us.

Just a few decades before I was born, Einstein changed how we think of time. Events that occur at one moment can be apparent to another person at a different time. His work is expressed in language that is difficult to understand, but his ideas have survived all tests. It is not necessary to know the details to appreciate that his are the ideas of a "modern" time that breaks out of the familiar and expected and is not constrained either by the ordinary or the magical.

I started to write about Time when I was in the hospital for a week with an infection triggered by a virus outbreak where we live. The doctor, Hatim Youssef, who came greeted me with "I was in your physics class as a pre-med, and you marked my life." He had failed the first test but liked the class and decided to take it more seriously. Here he was, one of the most liked and admired physicians in the hospital. A great illustration of magical time for me, and a time of breaking out of the ordinary with decisions toward the future for him.

* * * * *

I have now passed my 100th birthday and people sometimes remark on that. I answer that I am very fortunate and take no credit for it. I say that such matters are decided under higher authority, in an office to which I have no access.

My father died at 90 from an aneurysm. Up to that time he was active and healthy and thought he had a few more years of life left. He was surprised when he got weaker. I was there when he asked his doctor, "What is happening to me?" and she said, "It's called old age," which I thought was a really bad answer. Soon his heart would no longer let him move and walk as before. "*Dass mein Tod so aussehn soll ...*" he said to me. "That my death should look like this ..."

Cousin Herbert was a better role model. The son of one of my father's sisters, fifteen years older than I, he graduated as a Doctor of Medicine in Vienna, and he added a public health degree after he immigrated to the United States. The small office where he began as a county public health officer grew to become a major health facility in a building named in his honor. He also had a private practice and was a professor at the University of California. He didn't give up his participation in committees until he was 100 years old. He drove his wife Hanna to her dialysis sessions three times a week until she died at age 83, when he was 92.

The Unitarian Church he attended as an obstreperous nonbeliever put Hanna's name on a memorial wall. He was shown the empty space next to hers, and told, "This is for you." "I am not so eager," he countered, with the usual twinkle in his eye. He lived to 103, lucid until close to the end.

After Herbert's memorial service had gone on for a while, we were startled to hear his voice, clear, wise, and as wonderful as it had always been, coming over the loudspeaker in a recording that he had prepared for the occasion. "I can't be with you," he began, and went on to finish, "Death is part of life."

One of the last times that I saw him, in his middle 90s, was at a dance performance in that same church. He called it "movement" rather than dance, but in any case, it was remarkable. He was at the center of the performance. The others were young people who first turned away from him in rebellion, but then came together at the all-embracing end.

The awareness of the approach of death hasn't kept me from continuing my activities. I would like to finish these remembrances. I also want to clean up and organize what my heirs will have to confront.

* * * * *

My political activities continue to be important to me. Over the years I have been active in the Coalition for Peace Action and in J Street, the liberal Jewish organization that advocates for Middle East policies that make the region hospitable and peaceful for all who live there. It has worked for the rights of Palestinians in Israel and for the establishment of a neighboring state of their own.

My most substantial involvement has been with the Princeton Community Democratic Organization (PCDO). I was reminded of its beginnings when it celebrated its 50th anniversary in 2017, and it turned out I was the only one who had been there at its founding who was still active. It was a happy occasion, and I got a shout-out from New Jersey's newly elected governor.

In the intervening years the town has changed from electing only Republicans to reliably electing Democrats. Some of the transformation was the result of demographic changes, but the PCDO can take a share of the credit. In 2006, the group was dominated by members who were quite conservative, and I found myself again in opposition to the establishment, a member of an insurgent group. There was a strongly contested election which the progressive wing won, and the PCDO was back as the most active Democratic club in the state. I became the recording secretary and was reelected in each of the following seventeen years until I had to give up my membership when we left Princeton.

At the memorial service for a friend, I was startled to see Edith Piaf's song *Je ne regrette rien* printed on the program. Really? "I regret nothing"? To regret nothing seems like such a luxury. Every life takes many turns. Some are the result of decisions made for us by others, but many are our own. The basic ones decide the education, work, and relationships that shape our lives.

At many points, my life might have veered off in a completely different direction. Would I have chosen engineering and then physics if there had been no economic pressure? If I had felt free and secure to follow another path? I have sometimes asked myself whether other pursuits, perhaps in the social sciences, might have been a better fit. Or, if I really had felt free of all constraints, writing or photography.

As it turned out, I did manage to transcend the traditional boundaries of my field. This was primarily because I made educational activities a priority from the beginning. Should I have tried to do that to an even greater degree? There are institutions that would have made it easier, perhaps more congenial, with less opposition than I encountered. When I was about to graduate from Columbia, my earlier supervisor, Polykarp Kusch, who must have seen that I might not follow the usual path, told me about an opening at a liberal arts college then in its infancy. I didn't pursue that lead, and later turned down other opportunities. I thought Rutgers would give me scope to go in different directions. I wanted to play in the big leagues, and the alternatives seemed to mean giving that up. But was that really so? Could I have made something of a different environment? Did I stick with the path I was on because it seemed known and secure, and because I wasn't sufficiently adventurous?

Actually, this "safe" way wasn't such a bad choice. When I started at Rutgers, the school was limited in its offerings and outlook, and I didn't expect to stay there for my entire career. I could not have envisioned its transformation from a somewhat narrow and conservative colonial college to the major state university that it is today.

As an outsider during my high school years, I wanted to be like everyone else. To be accepted. To join the easy banter. It took me a long time to learn to strive beyond conformity.

I took some steps in my first university years, when I became interested in social and international problems, and turned away from nationalism and the glorification of any one ethnic group. During my first university year, I attended some Zionist meetings because of my friendship with Seemah, and I saw how comforting it was to be part of an idealistic, like-minded body of people. But I couldn't accept the exceptionalism, the premise of "we're better than they are" just because of where and to whom we were born.

Jews often consider themselves separate and special. Restrictions and persecutions have been a constant through the ages, leading to reactions like, "Dear God, we've been your chosen people for 5,000 years. Please, choose another one!" I am still repelled by rah-rah cheering for clan or country. I still see the connections rather than the differences as more important and more interesting.

* * * * *

I went through university without a mentor or role model who might have helped me avoid some mistakes. The only physicist I knew before I was on the road to becoming one was a refugee in Vancouver with a Viennese degree. His mission was to translate a well-known German textbook that was supposed to contain all of physics. Well, not exactly all, just "classical" physics, mostly what had been known before the end of the 19th century. He found a collaborator who helped him to accomplish it. I doubt it found many buyers.

Not until I had been at Rutgers for fifteen years did I meet Bob Kates, who taught me to look at the value of my activities and those of others more critically, and to search for contributions that were not likely to be made by others.

I can imagine different ways that my work could have

evolved. It is possible for me to think of a different environment. I have also speculated whether, with another partner, I could have avoided the kind of difficulties that Lore and I experienced. More often than not, I stayed with the cards I was dealt, perhaps because I needed a haven after the buffeting in my early life and exodus, the conflicts between my parents, and my unsteady schooling. I have looked for steadiness and, in part at least, I found it between the ups and downs of my roller-coaster life.

THE PARTY

When March 2020 came, Tom was going to be 65 and it was time for a party. When he was born, I was 30 years and 12 days old, and now we wanted to celebrate our birthdays together. We planned food, drink, and music. It was not to be. The threat of viral infection canceled every gathering.

As I think about that time, my mind wanders. I see the party starting: it's 1931, in Vienna, and I am six years old. I go down the stairs from the third floor and out of the building at *Hernalser Hauptsrasse* 78 and turn left. I cross the street and walk along the side of the square that opens up, the *Elterleinplatz,* to the corner of the *Kalvarienberggasse.* I turn right to go up the hill. Just past the church is my school, and there, in the large and anonymously gray classroom, is my first-grade teacher, *Lehrer Rosenkranz,* talking to us 40 boys in his class.

A while later I am with *Oberlehrerin Reiss* in the brightly lit and animated *Schwarzwaldschule.* In the group of children are Lisbeth and Ingmar, as we copy numbers and cut out pictures. Frau Reiss shows us how to cut: "Open the scissors wide, and close them all the way." *Tante Litschi* arrives with her two daughters. She advances toward me, shouting *Zwickipussi*! *Zwicken* is to pinch, and *Pussi* is diminutive for kiss. She squeezes my cheeks with her two hands and plants a kiss on my mouth. I am desperate to escape. My cousin Erika is in the hazy background, her younger sister Renate explores the room. When she first sees me, bundled up in the baby carriage, she says, "Sweet, sweet, and when does he grow legs?"

Now it's my friends from the Gymnasium, the time of grades five to seven, Tommy and Schurl. I see Tommy's mother as she starts a question when I sit down in their apartment in the Karl-Marx Hof for the snack that she offers.

The physics teacher comes by, Professor Ungar, and Dr. Gröger, the German teacher, with his tales of hardships in the mountains during the First World War.

Through the window I see some who are not invited: the Nazi classmates, the ones who greet each other each morning with their ostentatious heel-clicking and military manner, the ones who see themselves as the elite, the Aryan leaders destined to rule the world. The blind French teacher comes to the house with her Braille pin. And Max Feuermann behind her. He was my father's patient who gave me violin lessons, though he cringed in pain each time I tried to play a note, and my first foray into the musical world came to an end.

Here is Ida Halpern, a fellow refugee with a doctorate in music from Vienna. She gave me piano lessons, and I practiced on the piano in the high school gym. Ida and her husband were struggling. He was a chemist who found a process to make cod liver oil shed its widely hated smell and taste. I assisted him when he made pills that he tried to sell to local drug stores. It was not a promising approach. But the idea turned out to be good, and he got a job with the Canadian Fishing Company. In the end, he was able to give a substantial endowment to the retirement home where they spent their final years.

Ida did not find easy acceptance either, especially from the society women in the refugee community, who looked down on the accent and mannerisms of her Polish upbringing. But she developed a successful chamber music society, and recorded the music of the Canadian indigenous peoples, for which she received one of the highest Canadian government honors. It was a major contribution to her adopted homeland and another triumph of the underdog.

Lily walks in, the Viennese widow of a writer and philosopher. She found out about my interest in coins, developed from loose change acquaintances brought back from trips. She said, "I must show you my drachma." As soon as I saw it, I knew that it was a tetradrachm from the time of Alexander the Great, in excellent condition. I made a few notes about what I saw, and a few days later sent her a 14-page dissertation with the date when it was minted and where. I got the compliments I was fishing for, and years later she called to tell me that a dealer had offered her 400 dollars for the coin, but she would give it to me for 300. I didn't have 300 disposable dollars and reluctantly turned her down.

People from my later musical life are now streaming by. I was told that the recorder is an easy instrument and started to learn to play before we came to Princeton. I got a second recorder for Lore. She was practicing her first notes in the apartment when the landlady knocked on the ceiling from below: "Can you shut that thing off?!" Lore never touched it again.

I continued, playing with a group that met every few weeks with a teacher—here he is, Morris Newman, funny and direct, saying, "If music were better paid, you would be coming to me in New York, instead of my coming here." The imperious Mrs. Dana occasionally called me to play with her group when one of her regulars was missing. "You should really play with people at your own level," was one of her early comments.

And I did get better. I played the different-sized instruments with the Princeton Recorder Society, and later also with a quartet that turned into a quintet, meeting in different houses. It was an important part of my life for some decades.

The visitors continue, bringing back the time of the exodus. My mother's Italian family, cousin Guido's children, Renato and Dinah, whom I saw in their homes in Jerusalem, and then when they came to visit here. The children and the Sisters from the Swiss sanatorium. More vividly now, as we arrive in British Columbia in 1939, Aha's commanding presence, and her two teenage daughters, Lisl and Lore. But wait, I see the girls again as older women, in photographs by Lore's daughter Jenny, who is my last link to Aha, the remarkable woman responsible for our path to Canada.

Now the guests tumble past, increasing in numbers as the time gets closer to the present. Lives lived and lives derailed and unlived, with scenes of promise denied, as well as those of fulfilment, warmth, and love.

Hello, Jean! Do you remember when we were 15, and you taught me to walk protectively on the street side of the sidewalk? And now, Seemah, with your glow and your voice, I am transported to that lyrical year in Winnipeg. I embrace my friends from UBC. Let me call you Robert and Richard. You were the brightest and the best, both on the way to your futures when you became trapped in the snares of sex—one of you by a short-lived affair with a student; the other, after four children, leaving your family for a man, and dying of AIDS.

Here is Martin, the industrialist, a little stiff and hard to get to know—did you meet Elda as her patient? Do you remember when I had a record player and wanted a box for it? Elda said, "Why don't you ask Martin for some wood from his factory?" I did, and when I picked it up, it was like nothing I had ever seen, smooth and patterned birch, a jewel more than a piece of wood. I made a rough box. You asked to see it, and ran your finger along the rough and uneven edge. You didn't say a word, but I knew that I had desecrated the jewel, and still feel mortified.

Here are the friends from International House. Barbara, where are you now? And George. Bill Hardy—your name came up when I met the authors of de Kooning's biography. They have a couple of pages describing what they know of your relationship with de Kooning's wife Elaine. I remember her painting in your apartment above your bed. You took me up the narrow stairs to the loft on 8th Street, to John Cage's talk, the "non-lecture" as it was later called. I wonder where life took you.

Columbia. Fellow students. Victor? Still in your lab coat in the basement of Columbia's physics building, under the hood that I never trusted, filling the metal box with powdered beryllium, probably more hazardous than all the radioactivity that we used in our experiments. A small army of professors: Kusch and Rabi. C.S. Wu, in your narrow Chinese dress, formal, and totally into your experiment. I could have asked to work with you. Much might have evolved differently, but in what direction?

Others have faded into facelessness.

Mr. Donaldson: you helped me with the equipment at Drew University. I still cherish your wedding present, the two silver candlesticks, and memories of your kindness.

Not everybody followed in the grooves that seemed to be laid out for them. Bill, you were a professor with the kind of job that's considered most desirable in our line of work. You left for a less well-known university, where I was happy to help you celebrate your 90th birthday not long ago. And John, you were at RCA, the pioneering TV company, and left for a university position. Did they expect you to continue on the same path? You set up a lab to study the movement of algae, and were still doing that when I flew to welcome you to the society of nonagenarians.

Hello, Maggi! Before we moved to Princeton, you said we must get into Mrs. Smith's nursery school. Do you remember, Neave, the day when I was "helping father" and you came to sit on my lap and asked, "Are you a daddy? We don't have a daddy," and you told me about your four siblings. Here is your mother, to whom I felt close. Your memorial meeting, Helen, with all five children, now grown, was held at the isolated house on the rock promontory jutting out into the ocean on the Rhode Island coast. You were described as the great mother and cook and homemaker, but that's not how I remember you: you were a biologist before you became that mother. You saw the world with the insight of knowledge, and our times together and our conversations remain with me.

Here is Peggy with George and their children, also from the nursery school. You invited us to spend some vacation days with you on Cape Cod. We collected clams for a clambake and marveled at your family unity, while Lore and I were less than harmonious. But you left him, saying that he was unfeeling and remote. He remarried, but you were left alone, while our rocky marriage survived.

* * * * *

When we moved into our house, Vincent, the owner of the lot north of us, an electrician, was working on his house. The rest of the space was empty. So was the large area south of the brook. It was the outskirts of town. Now it is full, and we feel we're close to the center of town. Of the six houses on our block, only that of Vincent was always owned by people born in America. Others were from China, Japan, France, Austria,

Germany and the Philippines. When houses were built farther down, many were those of immigrant families from Italy. Later, there were three that belonged to African Americans, among the first outside the neighboring area that is now designated a historic district to preserve the memory of its heritage as it changes and is absorbed into today's homogeneity.

The signs of transition are everywhere. Small houses are being torn down to make way for large and more expensive ones. Gentrification is pushing out the less affluent and minority populations. How to control and channel the changes has become the dominant question of town politics. At one time, I needed to have the house appraised. The parting words of the appraiser were, "You know what's going to happen when this house is sold, don't you? It will be torn down!" I said I hoped I wouldn't be there to see that.

There were times that were very positive and times that were not. And that's how life continued. At Rutgers. With Lore. With the children. I liked being fully in life, even when it was difficult. I liked to work. And I still do.

As you all pass by in my memory, I relive my life. I hesitate to use the word *love* but I have feelings of love for so many of you, each in a different way. Even those of you who caused me difficulties contributed to my life.

* * * * *

I shake myself loose from my dream. The party that did not happen morphs into the one that took place just a short time ago, on my hundredth birthday.

People congratulate me, but what have I done? I have been given a gift of time. I answer that I am very fortunate and take no credit for it. I say that such matters are decided under higher authority, in an office to which I have no access.

Have I used my gift wisely? Perhaps sometimes. I think of the times when I have not, but who can say what a step in another direction might have led to? I have been at the edge of precipices. And there have been times of pleasure, success, and joy. I have been myself, and there is no one for whose life I would want to exchange mine.

My father died at 90 from an aneurysm. Up to that time, he was active and healthy and thought he had a few more years of life left. He was surprised when he got weaker. I was there when he asked his doctor, "What is happening to me?" and she said, "It's called old age," which I thought was a really bad answer. Soon his heart would no longer let him move and walk as before. *Dass mein Tod so aussehn soll* ... he said to me. "That my death should look like this ..."

Cousin Herbert was a better role model. The son of one of my father's sisters, 15 years older than I, he graduated as a Doctor of Medicine in Vienna, and added a public-health degree after he immigrated to the United States. The small office where he began as a county public health officer grew to become a major health facility in a building named in his honor. He also had a private practice and was a professor at the University of California. He didn't give up his participation in committees until he was 100 years old. He drove his wife Hanna to her dialysis sessions three times a week until she died at age 83, when he was 92.

The Unitarian Church he attended as an obstreperous nonbeliever put Hanna's name on a memorial wall. He was shown the empty space next to hers, and told, "This is for you."

"I am not so eager," he countered, with the usual twinkle in his eye. He lived to 103, lucid until close to the end.

After Herbert's memorial service had gone on for a while, we were startled to hear his voice, clear, wise, and as wonderful as it had always been, coming over the loud- speaker in a recording that he had prepared for the occasion. "I can't be with you," he began, and went on to finish, "Death is part of life."

One of the last times that I saw him, in his middle 90s, was at a dance performance in that same church. He called it "movement" rather than dance, but in any case, it was remarkable. He was at the center of the performance. The others were young people who first turned away from him in rebellion, but then came together at the all-embracing end.

I am not afraid of death, and the awareness of its approach hasn't kept me from continuing my activities. I would like to finish these remembrances. And continue, as long as I can, to observe, and to participate.

Again, my mind veers to those who were not there: My parents, Elda and Bela, and Lore. The relationships were sometimes great. I wish I could have avoided the more difficult times, but as the song says, there is no replay in the game of life.

* * * * *

At the party, my children talked with a warmth that enveloped me, and so did Mary. Most of those who said something were part of the extended family. But the first was Stewart Smith, whose background is far from mine, growing up in rural Manitoba, breaking the traditions of his family, marrying Norma, a nurse from Sweden. He became a major physicist and administrator at Princeton University.

Chiara Nappi knew me from another angle and mentioned my activities with political groups, including J Street, the liberal Jewish group, whose meetings often took place in her house.

She was followed by Phyllis, who was a neighbor, and now is again. She reminded me what influence distance has. When I moved away from Vancouver, I lost the context of my life with its friendships. Only a few could be continued, and those only weakly. Lore hoped we would settle in California because of the people she knew there. We move around more easily than we used to, but even small distances separate us.

Earlier in this story, when we talked about Lore's time at Black Mountain College, you met her friend Lisa Aronson, and here, at the party, is her son Marc with his wife Marina Budhos. The friendship continues through the generations, now with their two sons Sasha and Rafi. I have known Marc since his first days, and he talks about me as an uncle and now grandfather figure to his family. Marina follows him and reminisces about holidays that we have spent together. Both of them are authors and Marina has taken on the task of helping me as this story comes together.

Most of my former students were too far away to be here. Only Youzhu and his wife are nearby. They like to see the world and go far from their house here as well as from their apartment in Beijing.

Others are here in spirit. Milind is in South Carolina. He changed his work only recently from superconductivity to the perception of sound. He got numerous awards for his teaching and is writing a book about that experience. I had a part in mentoring 20 PhD students from different countries. Talso, who did some of the most precise temperature measurements done, started in Cambodia. Not so many Americans, but one was Tom Greenslade, who built an addition to his house for the old apparatus that he collected and wrote about. He retired with an honorary degree, and the Millikan award that I mentioned earlier. There is also Gordon Aubrecht who might have had that kind of recognition, but died prematurely.

I am struck by the flow of generations. Here is Lily, Mary's granddaughter. What an accomplished young woman. What is most special for me is that without any prompting she made the effort to be here for the celebration. She was the youngest of those who spoke, and her spontaneous words were a special gift.

Tom's son Sam is here, an adult now, with a degree from art school, illustrating and painting in his own distinctive style, making his way, and teaching kids that are troubled but respond to the directness of what he does with them with paint and brush.

From a different part of the family, there is Susan, the daughter of Lore's brother Kurt, who came with her husband Jack, her two children, and two of her grandchildren. She talked about the importance of family, and you had to know her well to realize that there were dark corners in her own memories, including those of her parents' refugee experience, which was related to that of my family, and at the same time quite different. Kurt grew up in his father's business world, which was presumably the successor to the legendary world of the door-to-door peddler of still earlier times.

All signs point to that world also as the place where my grandfather Moritz started. One of his five children (my father) went off into a world that was more modern and more intellectual, through the study of medicine. This was also the path taken by Moritz's grandson Herbert, who was part of my generation.

A third path was taken by Lore when she studied art, and left her parents for Black Mountain College.

As I listened, I thought of the strength of character that it took. For each the path was new, without a mentor or model, and without much of the encouragement that might have helped. When Susan's children had children of their own, there was no doubt that she would be there, first with diapers, later with school assignments. "That's what my mother did for me," she said.

That's the spirit we need to nourish, whether we're alone, members of a nuclear or extended family, or part of the small or large group of citizens of the world. Being there, with others, and for others, is what it's all about. That's what I mean by being liberal, or progressive. That's the direction, and the touchstone.

Did my story describe just me and my experiences? Or also a time, and places, and the paths of many? Did you encounter moods that are familiar to you? Perhaps what you read took you to where you had been, to struggles that you had, on stretches of the journey that we shared, the smooth and the rough, the predictable, and the bolts out of the blue.

I am writing at a time of change. The virus pandemic of 2020 triggered some of it, leading to difficult times, and also to the efforts of vaccination, which brought the country back to health. When a great need is seen, it will no longer be possible to say "it can't be done." To avoid progress on a problem, we can say "we don't want it" or "we don't want it badly enough," but we have seen what can be achieved when political will is mobilized.

Today's political crisis as I write in 2025 is tearing the country apart. My experience and my faith in the strength of people and institutions lead me to expect a restoration of the former values.

The old labels of conservative, progressive, and reactionary, left and right, do not describe us well. I see changes in the air that will bring new groupings, different alignments, perhaps new thoughts.

On one side are those whose circle of concern is narrow and looking inward, to themselves, their family, their tribe.

The great division is between them and those who see the connections between all of us, our interdependence, the need for all to thrive and to care for each other.

What are our economic and political systems for, if not to make it possible to work together to better the lives of all, as we share the riches that the earth gives us?

The old slogans won't do. The old categories put us in boxes that no longer fit. What are we doing to change people's lives in this country and in the world for the better and to preserve the environment of which we are the custodians?

I don't embrace everybody. Not those who have brought us to the present inequality of wealth in the face of pervasive poverty. Not those who have fostered a poverty of spirit.

I don't think we are going back to how things were, to the comfort of what we are used to. The opportunities are unlimited. How will we use them?

I'll leave you there, with the words of my mother's mentor Alfred Adler, when he left for his last journey: *Macht's gut, Kinder!* Literally, "Do it well, children," with its universal meaning.

Good luck to all of us. For a new and better time.

END NOTES

1. This weekly program has been hosted by John Weingart since 1974 on the radio station WPRB, Princeton, NJ. For most of that time, John was the Associate Director of the Eagleton Institute of Politics at Rutgers University.

2. The history of this experiment can be followed in four publications. The first is: Peter Lindenfeld, "Size effects in conductivity and superconductivity," *The Physics Teacher*, vol. 18, p. 260, April 1980. This is an informal article with the most readable description of this work. It is reprinted on the website <firstscience.rutgers.edu>. The second is a technical article: T. Worthington, P. Lindenfeld, and G. Deutscher, "Heat Capacity Measurements of the Critical Coupling between Aluminum Grains," *Physical Review Letters*, vol. 41, p. 316, 1978. A third article is more comprehensive: R. L. Filler, P. Lindenfeld, T. Worthington, and G. Deutscher, "Heat Capacity Measurements of Granular Aluminum," *Physical Review B*, vol. 21, p. 5031, 1980. It leaves open the possibility of the validity of a publication by a member of Guy's lab (reference 26), which assumed that the grains remained superconducting, but that the path of the electrons went in and out of the grains. We had measured the heat capacity of our specimens, and her curves of that quantity as the temperature changed were so similar to the ones we observed that they could not be ignored.

The whole point of our work seemed to be questioned. Were the isolated grains superconducting or not? We had thought that the superconductivity had disappeared in the individual grains because they were too small. The new calculation seemed to show that the grains remained superconducting.

To show that this was not so, Milind Kunchur made more detailed measurements as a function of temperature and magnetic field. He showed that there was a region where the grains were separate, metallic, and not superconducting. The resulting paper's title said it all: M. Kunchur, P. Lindenfeld, W. L. McLean, and J. S. Brooks, "Absence of Superconductivity in Metallic Granular Aluminum," *Physical Review Letters,* vol. 59, p. 1232, 1987. Our initial conclusion was correct. Our grains were too small to exhibit the bulk property of superconductivity.

3. A biographical essay about Lore, with an illustrated catalog of her work, was published in 1997 as No. 3 in the series "Black Mountain College Dossiers" by the Black Mountain College Museum and Arts Center, Asheville, North Carolina. "Lore Kadden Lindenfeld: A Life in Textiles, 1945–1997," by Sigrid Wortmann Weltge, Professor of Art and Design History at the Philadelphia College of Textiles and Science, now Philadelphia University + Thomas Jefferson University.

4. Millikan Lecture 1989: Peter Lindenfeld, "The Einsteinization of Physics," *American Journal of Physics*, vol. 58, p. 301, 1990. Also at < firstscience.rutgers.edu>.

5. This thought is echoed in an essay by Rush Holt, whose theme is that science and scientists have allowed themselves to become detached and remote from the public to the detriment of all. Rush Holt, "Companion Essay to the 75th anniversary reprint of the influential report," in *Science, The Endless Frontier*, by Vannevar Bush, Princeton University Press, 2021. Rush Holt was our congressman from 1999 to 2015, and later the head of the American Association for the Advancement of Science. I was a volunteer and occasional driver for him in his early campaigns. On election evening, November 1998, some of us left his headquarters when he seemed to have lost, but raced back when it was announced that an error had been made. From then on, New Jersey's 12th congressional district has been fortunate to be represented by him and his successor, Bonnie Watson Coleman.

6. George Pallrand and Peter Lindenfeld, "The physics classroom revisited: Have we learned our lesson?" *Physics Today,* v. 38 No. 11, p. 46, Nov 1985.

7. Peter Lindenfeld, "From New Brunswick to Tirupati with PSSC," in *PSSC: 50 Years Later*, AAPT, 2006. Available at: https://www.compadre.org/portal/pssc/docs/Lindenfeld.pdf

8. Robert March. *Physics for Poets*, McGraw-Hill, 2002.

9. Peter Lindenfeld and Suzanne White Brahmia. *Physics: The First Science*, Rutgers University Press, 2011. The book is now out of print, but is freely available on the website <firstscience.rutgers.edu>.

10. Kathy Shan, *American Journal of Physics*, v. 80, p. 1115, 2012; John L. Roeder, *The Physics Teacher*, v. 50, p. 318, 2012; Shaukat Goderya, *Physics Today*, July 2012. There is also an interview with Suzanne and me in *Physics Today*, July 10, 2012. These reviews and interview are freely available on the website <firstscience.rutgers.edu>.

11. Naomi's work can be seen on her Facebook page NaomiLindenfeldColoredClay. The following publications have illustrations of her work:

    Studio Potter magazine, January 1995.
    Ceramics Monthly magazine, September 1996.
    Kathy Triplett. *Handbuilt Ceramics*. Lark Press, 1998.
    Jane Waller. *Colour in Clay*. Crowood Press, 1998.
    Jo Connell. *Colouring Clay*. University of Pa. Press, 2007.
    Ceramics Monthly magazine, January 2016.
    Working with Porcelain, Ceramic Arts Network.

TIMELINE

B. March 10, 1925, Vienna, Austria.
Mother: b. Elda Lachs 1897, Trieste (Italy),
d. 1967 in Vancouver at age 70.
Father: b. Bela 1882, Budapest (Hungary),
d. 1972 in Vancouver at age 90.

Hernalser Hauptstrasse 78, Vienna, 1925–1938.
Elementary schools:
Volksschule, Kalvarienberggasse, 1931–1932.
Schwarzwaldschule 1932–1935.
Gymnasium: *Gymnasium* of the 18th district (G18), 1935–1938. Spring 1938: Chajes Gymnasium, to which all Jewish students were transferred.

Anschluss: Invasion and takeover of Austria by Germany, March 11, 1938.

Left Vienna in April for Trieste.

Sanatorium des Enfants, Leysin, Switzerland, 1938–1939.

Tunbridge Wells, England, 1939.

Southampton to Montreal, Canada, on *Duchess of Atholl*. Sooke, Vancouver Island, British Columbia. 1939.

Vancouver, King George High School, 1939–1941, graduation 1941.

Lampshade factory, office jobs, correspondence courses for grade 13 (equivalent to first year college), 1941–42.

University of Manitoba, Winnipeg, 1942–1943. Mother in Manitoba (Winnipeg and Brandon) 1941–1943. Father arr. Vancouver 1942.

University of British Columbia (UBC) 1943–1948, Bachelor of Applied Science in Electrical Engineering, 1946. Master of Applied Science in Engineering Physics, 1948.
Graduate student and teaching assistant,
Physics Department, 1946–48. Summer 1948:
Chalk River (Canada's nuclear reactor and laboratory).

Columbia University, teaching assistant 1948–1950, research assistant 1950–1952, PhD 1954. New York, International House, 1948–1950, apartment (119th Street), shared with George Schillinger, 1950–1952.

Lore Kadden: met 1950, married May 31, 1953 in Earl Hall, Columbia University. d. 2010. Children: Thomas b. 1955, Naomi b. 1958.

Visiting lecturer, Physics Department, Drew University, Madison, NJ, 1952–1953.

Rutgers University, New Brunswick and Piscataway, NJ:

Instructor 1953–1955, Assistant Professor 1955–1961, Associate Professor 1961–1966, Professor 1966–1982, Professor II (later called Distinguished Professor) 1982–1999, Professor Emeritus and member of the Graduate School to present.

New York, 89th Street, 1953, North Brunswick, NJ, 1953–1955, Highland Park, NJ, 1955–1957, Princeton, NJ, 1957–present.

1962, England (Eynsham and Oxford).

1965, Tirupati, India (program of Agency for International Development). Conferences on low-temperature physics and superconductivity, England, France, Finland, USSR, Germany, Israel, Japan, USA, side trips to Austria, Holland, Switzerland, Spain, Italy, Turkey.

1970–1971, France (Paris and University of Paris, Orsay).

1980, Visiting Scholar, Kyoto University, Japan.

Fellow, American Physical Society. American Association of Physics Teachers (AAPT): fellow, honorary member NJ Section. 1988 Warren I. Susman Award for Excellence in Teaching, Rutgers University. 1989 Robert A. Millikan lecture award and medal, AAPT. 2011 *Physics, The First Science,* Rutgers University Press.

ACKNOWLEDGMENTS

This book reflects the century of my life, with its times of stability and those of uncertainty. It was shaped by all whom I encountered, none more than my mother, who early on recognized the danger we were in, and whose determination allowed her to escape Nazi-occupied Austria with me, and later also to save my father.

When I complained about being bullied by a classmate whose name was Benno, she surprised me by saying "There will always be a Benno," trying to transmit to me the resilience in the face of challenges and obstacles that characterized her life.

My children taught me from their first days, and are continuing to do so, each following paths different from the other, and from their parents. Past being children, they are now supporters, advisors, and friends, joined by Naomi's husband Michael Bosworth, Tom's partner Becky Leise, and my partner Mary's son Will Clurman.

Lore, in our marriage of 57 years, had the children that both of us wanted. She taught me to see with her artist's eyes, and was my companion for the largest part of my life. Mary Clurman is my loyal partner as we travel through the following years.

During my work on a preliminary edition I had the help of Gail Wurst. Her comments did much to create the shape of the narrative.

The debt to my teachers is evident in what I wrote. It is joined to the debt to my students.

Marina Budhos, friend, teacher, and writer, took a special interest in the book, and made many formative suggestions and contributions.

I am grateful to Jessica Powers and Catalyst Press for publishing the book, joined by Henry Trotter. Will Clurman has had an important role in every aspect. Their work and their encouragement have been invaluable.

A book is the product of many people, and I am fortunate to have had the support that has made this one possible. My thanks go to all who have been part of the process.

Peter Lindenfeld, July 2025

www.ingramcontent.com/pod-product-compliance
Lightning Source LLC
Jackson TN
JSHW020419201225
95650JS00005B/1
9781963511321